Bridegroom's Song

Before Creation, There Was God's Bridal Song

Bride's Heart

Becoming The Bride Of Christ

Debra Webster

FREEDOM IS OUR BIRTHRIGHT

Bride's Heart — Becoming The Bride Of Christ

5 STEPS TO A TRANSFORMED MIND

GAL. 5:1 FOR FREEDOM CHRIST HAS SET US FREE

Click this link or type in your search bar for your free book.

https://www.bridesheart.com/

Published by His Glory Publishing
P.O. Box 20296
Indianapolis, IN 46220-0296
https://Bridesheart.com

Copyright © 2014 Debra Webster
First Edition Printing 2014
Second Edition Printing 2023
Third Edition Printing 2024
All rights reserved.
ISBN10:0692026649
ISBN13:978-0-692026649

DEDICATION

This book is dedicated to my family who walked with me, loving me as I learned the lessons of Song of Songs. This was especially true of my husband George, who modeled the love of the Bridegroom Lamb to me.

Also, I dedicate this to my mother, who upheld our family in prayer through all these years until the Lord took her to glory in 2014. Though the poem Intercessor included in the manuscript was not written specifically about her, it describes the destiny she fulfilled in this earth and for our family.

I dedicate this as well to the Bride of His Heart. She exists within the "church" listening for His voice. She is the reason I write and the reason He died.

To see more books and read about them, click the first link.

http://www.amazon.com/author/debrawebster

To go to the website, click the next link.
https://www.bridesheart.com/

CONTENTS

ACKNOWLEDGEMENTS

Thanks first to my family, who lived this experience with me and helped me survive the process. Special thanks to my daughter Crista who helped edit the manuscript.

Thanks also go to Carol Radigan, who helped me overcome the results of the wounding years, so I could fulfill the rest of my destiny in this world.

Darryl and Patty, thank you for coming faithfully to bible study as I taught out of this manuscript that I wrote 20 years previously. God used you to reactivate the gift that had been long buried.

Thanks to those who were part of the wounding. Without you the cry of my heart to know the Bridegroom would never have been realized.

Bridegroom's Song

Preface

Many years ago, I started on a quest to know God. The impetus for this quest came out of great frustration with the contradictory teachings circulating within the Lord's church. I wanted the truth, and to embrace truth, I knew I must come to know God. The scripture became my only resource for truth, and the desire in my heart to know Him was my main safeguard against error. This led me to develop a method of study I use today.

Life experience taught me an image of God that was not truth. The church, often by its actions and sometimes by its teachings, reinforced my distorted image of God. I felt awash in a sea of confusion worshipping a caricature of God. I realized I did not see Him as He is. As the desire to know Him became the driving force of my life, the rest fell into place. "Bridegroom's Song" results from that quest. First studied that I might apprehend Him, I later taught it as a bible study. The fruit in the lives of this author and those present was surprising. It became apparent that God had further purposes for the things He taught me. Many urged me to write this book for the Lord's church.

This study took place over a four-year period. During that time, I went through Song of Songs three times. I studied each word in the original language. The context of the Song and the passage determined the meaning when contradictions existed among authorities. I am not a theologian but studied each word in the context of the Song of Songs, and in harmony with the rest of scripture. For example, when studying wine, I compared it with every other use of wine in the word. The conclusions drawn harmonize with the whole bible and the context.

Intimacy with the Bridegroom.

I know many interpret this book as the relationship between a man and his wife. This is a valid interpretation and an important one. Many of the passages in Song of Songs are helpful to married couples. Because of a lack of understanding in the church today about preparing the bride of His heart, I wrote this manuscript from that viewpoint. The church needs a deeper relationship with Him. This deeper relationship is the purpose of Song of Songs.

Though not a theologian, I am a seeker of God and as a seeker, I share this with you. Perhaps you are tired of the confusing voices around you. What you will find in reading this is God. That is the entire purpose for writing this book. I cannot vouch that every word within is perfect, but if you want to meet with God, I believe with my whole heart, you will find Him here. I did. It was in studying this one book I came to love Him in a way I did not know was possible. I do not say this because my writing is wonderful, but because Song of Songs itself is life changing.

In eternity past there was only God. The fellowship between the three persons of the Trinity was and is perfect. The love shared beyond description. God decided He wanted to share this love with a being created in His image.

Before God created the world for man, God knew He had to become a man and die to redeem the man He created. The message of Song of Songs helps us understand why He created us despite this.

Man became the object of His love. God gave us marriage to help us understand the closeness of divine fellowship. Then He told us He was coming back to earth for a bride, and He would help prepare us for this close relationship.

The custom of the Jewish bridegroom of Jesus day was for the bridegroom to sing a song in honor of the bride at the wedding. Song of Songs is our Bridegroom's song in honor of His bride. It is the greatest love story of all time. He has been singing this song over His bride since before He created man. Song of Songs reveals the greatest love of the ages. That love is for us.

If you are tired of confusion or need to know Him as He is then this book is for you. Would you like to make sense of the pain, persecution, and challenges? Then this book is for you. Are you successful beyond belief or able to control your world to keep out the pain or confusion? This book may not be for you.

Song of Songs takes the bride from first blush of romance to real maturity. The bride learns to come into His presence step by step. Just as the Jewish temple brought worshippers into the court, and the priests into the Holy Place and then the Holy of Holies, Song of Songs brings the bride into the presence of the King who loves her. But this takes place step-by-step. This Song describes a relationship between our Bridegroom and us that is decades in the making. That means the truths in Song of Songs unfold with more understanding as time passes. In a few months or years, a unique part of the manuscript will speak to you because your growth helps you understand the next step.

In Song of Songs the bride is a worshipper, a warrior, a dancer, and a slave. She is complacent, beautiful, who He saw as He died and everything He desires. This imagery is described by the Bridegroom in Song of Songs.

She is the reason God created us. The fellowship of the Father, Son and Holy Spirit is for us, too. His bride is getting ready for this fellowship.

He has chosen us to be His. He is complete without us, yet He wants us for His own.

Oh, Love that wilt not let me go.
I hide my weary soul in Thee.
I pay thee back the life I owe.
That in Thine ocean depth
Its flow may richer, fuller be. (Public Domain)

Chapter 1

The Corridor

There is a corridor in time with my name on it. The walls and ceilings are high, with lots of room for reverberations. Reverberations can hurt.

Darkness filled the corridor and extinguished hope's light..

Suddenly there appeared the brilliant white light of a cross. What hope, what glory flooded that place? A new start and a new finish lay before me. The love I felt defied description. How I rejoiced, unaware the darkness would return. Black swirling clouds filled the corridor as voices screamed:

"You are responsible for what went wrong"

"You are always wrong. I am always right."

"It is your responsibility to make everyone happy."

"Nothing will ever change. Your life will always be like this. There is no hope."

"You are too much."

"You are not enough."

"You must perform to be loved."

"God doesn't love you. If God loved you, your life wouldn't be so awful."

"God doesn't allow suffering. If you are hurting, it proves you are out of God's will or don't have enough faith."

"God has a baseball bat just for you. When you step out of line, He cracks you over the head."

"I am your authority. You must submit. Submit! Submit!"

Voices of the church, voices of my pain, voices of the past ricocheting and reverberating off the walls of my life, bouncing, striking, disabling, wounding. Fifteen years after that first glimpse of the cross, God spoke. *"You will know the Bridegroom, and what it means to be the bride, to the depth you suffered."*

God understood the flaming desire of my heart was to know Him. This passion kept me persevering. Now He was telling me that the purpose of the pain was, so I will love Him deeply, to the depth I had suffered. Fifteen years of darkness and vanquished hope now had purpose.

The pain did not end here as I hoped. Before He allowed the healing, I was desperate for; He tested the lessons He taught me. It was incomprehensible that the pain was so deep He hid me for 21 years to give me time to heal. Time showed I needed to forget everything I thought I knew and let Him remake me in an image of His creating. I did not grasp how much more death I had to die before His life would reign in me. I am still learning to take up my cross daily and receive His life.

This is my story. Your story is here and most of all, His story. My story plays a small part of this writing. His story is the main one, and yours is here by identification with my story and His. Your story is also here because Song of Songs is not a book to read, but a life to live. If you have been really living, you will understand the Song.

You will understand unless you live to avoid pain.
Unless you keep in the darkness
what only God can heal
when brought to light.
Unless you spend life hiding
in that case|
this will seem like foolishness.

Chapter 2

The Lord's Song

Family Slavery

It is a matter of slavery. Yes, you read right, slavery. "Whose slavery?" you ask? It is the bride's slavery. And my slavery, and yours. Song of Songs has a lot to teach us about slavery and death and life and love. "Strange," you say. It is not strange at all. Some of the mightiest acts God did began with slavery. Before we consider slavery, however, there must be an introduction.

What is Song of Songs, anyway? What makes Song of Songs so special?

Song 1:1 "The Song of Songs, which is Solomon's." KJV.

The title alone shows us it is a song above all other songs. The name Song of Songs comes from the first two words of the Hebrew text. It means the superlative, the song above all other songs. We see this device throughout scripture. One example is the Holy of Holies. This is the holy place above all holy places. Song of Songs describes the journey into the Secret Place, the innermost chambers: the Holy of Holies of the King of Kings and Lord of Lords. This book describes His bride and shows who He is in relation to her. It includes His kingship, His lordship, and His sacrifice that purchased her as His bride. His life was her bridal price. And she was the joy He saw, the joy set before Him as he died to purchase her. All of this is included in Song of Songs. In fact, the Lord has given a higher place to no other song. It is His song, the one He has been singing over His bride from the foundation of the world.

So why is this book called Solomon's Song? For Song of Songs to be written it had to be experienced. Solomon experienced this and then, under the inspiration of the Holy Spirit, wrote about it. Likewise, this is how Hosea wrote the book bearing his name.

Hosea and God

Hosea 1:2 'When the Lord began to speak through Hosea, the Lord said to him, "Go, take to yourself an adulterous wife and children of unfaithfulness, because the land is guilty of the vilest adultery in departing from the Lord."'

The prophet Hosea married Gomer, the harlot, who bore three children. Other men fathered some or all these children. The Lord, referring to the nation of Israel, for example, speaks in Hosea 2:4-5 *"I will not show my love to her children, because they are children of adultery. Their mother has been unfaithful and has conceived them in disgrace."*

Hosea named their first child Jezreel because God would judge the nation of Israel in the valley of Jezreel. He named the second child LO-ruhamah. This means "no compassion or no love"[i] for God would no longer show the Israelites mercy. The third child, God, called Lo-ammi. This means "not my people or not mine"[ii] for God, no longer claimed Israel as his people. (Hosea 1:3-9) This meant that this child was not Hosea's, but another man's.

Hosea 3:1-5 'The Lord said to me, "Go, show your love to your wife again, though she is loved by another and is an adulteress. Love her as the Lord loves the Israelites, though they turn to other gods and love the sacred raisin cakes." So, I bought her for about fifteen shekels of silver and about a lethek of barley. Then I told her, "you are to live with me many days; you must not be a prostitute or be intimate with any man, and I will live with you." For the Israelites will live many days, without king or prince, without sacrifice or sacred stones, without ephod or idol. Afterward, the Israelites will return and seek the Lord their God and David their king. They will come trembling to the Lord and to his blessings in the last days.'

Hosea's wife was unfaithful to him like the Israelites were to God. Just as Hosea bought back his own wife, similarly God bought back His people. This happened when Jesus made the ultimate sacrifice and died buying us back from sin.

Hosea lived God's experience and then wrote about it, so we could understand God's heart for His erring people. Solomon's purpose was to live out the relationship between the Bridegroom and the bride and write about it. This song was Solomon's song above all other songs, but it was first, last and forever God's preeminent song.

Many scholars consider Solomon as a type of the heavenly Bridegroom. The value of this book is not what it teaches us about Solomon, but what it teaches us concerning God. The story of Solomon and Shulamite has deep spiritual significance for those who desire to experience the Lord as their Bridegroom.

Shulamite and Jezebel

For example: Shulamite lived this experience. Without her and the bride there is no song. Shulamite was a young woman who came from the plain of Jezreel. This is the area in Israel mentioned in Hosea 1 as a place of judgment for the Israelites, better known as Armageddon. iii Many wars have taken place there. She came from a land of many battles and ultimate judgment. So has His bride. Do you feel as if you had many battles and judgments? Then you qualify to know Him as Bridegroom.

There is more to understand about Shulamite's birthplace. Jezreel was home to Jezebel, the wicked wife of Ahab, king of Israel. I list five of her wicked deeds below:

Jezebel had the owner of a vineyard killed so King Ahab could have it (1 Kings 21).

She worshipped Baal, god of the Phoenicians, and demanded that the Israelites do likewise.

Jezebel killed God's prophets (1 Kings 18).

No less than 400 prophets of Astarte and 450 prophets of Baal ate at her table (1 Kings 16: 31,32, I Kings 2:18-19).

Worship to Baal included human sacrifice and sexual temple rites.

Jezebel is the opposite of the bride. The name Jezebel means "unconsummated or un-husbanded".iii She can never be the bride. The bride experiences spiritual consummation halfway through Song of Songs. Jezebel married because as a king's daughter she must. However, she planned to rule through her husband Ahab. She never comprehended what it meant to be a vulnerable bride because she never let her husband be a true husband (1Ki.21: 5-23).

The Bible gives us pictures of two women, the bride and the harlot. Jezebel is a type of the harlot. Her end time description is in Rev. 17:1-18:3.

In this description, the Lord tells His people to come out of the Harlot. This means we cooperate with this false system.

We often exhibit more characteristics of the harlot than we do the bride, (more about this later). The enemy worked in our lives before we made Jesus Lord, and we need freedom. In fact, we are drawn toward the tendencies listed above daily when we first receive Him because old habits take time to replace. Over time He purges these things from our lives if we will let Him. Song of Songs illustrates the journey from harlot tendencies to fidelity.

Revelation's Harlot and Bride
The same angel that tells us of the judgment on the harlot I Revelation 17, shows us the Bride, the wife of the Lamb. The Lamb created the world to bring forth this bride. He lived as a man and died for His bride. The description that follows is what we are called to. It is the opposite from the Harlots.

Rev. 21:1 "Then I saw a new heaven and a new earth, for the first heaven and the first earth had passed away, and there was no longer any sea.

Rev. 21:2 I saw the Holy City, the new Jerusalem, coming down out of heaven from God, prepared as a bride beautifully dressed for her husband.

Rev. 21:9 One of the seven angels who had the seven bowls full of the seven last plagues came and said to me, "Come, I will show you the bride, the wife of the Lamb."

Rev. 21:10 And he carried me away in the Spirit to a mountain great and high, and showed me the Holy City, Jerusalem, coming down out of heaven from God.

Rev. 21:11 It shone with the glory of God, and its brilliance was like that of a very precious jewel, like jasper, clear as crystal.

Rev. 21:22 I did not see a temple in the city, because the Lord God Almighty and the Lamb are its temple.

Rev. 21:23 The city does not need the sun or the moon to shine on it, for the glory of God gives it light, and the Lamb is its lamp."

This description of the bride illustrates we are called to become this bride, the wife of the Lamb. Is it any wonder that our preparation is difficult and time consuming? How could it be less? We are exchanging what we call life for real life? The Lamb Himself and the glory of the Father illumine the city, His bride. The bride moves from harlot tendencies to the Lord becoming her light. Song of Songs shows this process.

Shulamite and Jezebel lived in the same place at different times. There is within each of us the ability to choose to be the harlot or the bride as our mental idols clamor for our attention.. Our Lord purchases us out of our harlotry when we fall into it, as Hosea did with his wife she had suffered much. Thus, suffering is the vehicle by which we give up our harlot tendencies to become His holy bride. Slavery and suffering help us make the right choice. The cross is always the path to glory. Our cross brings us into His glory and transforms us.

Shulamite was of the tribe of Issachar. Genesis 49:14-15 *"Issachar is a rawboned donkey lying down between two saddlebags. When he sees how good is his resting place and how pleasant is his land, He will bend his shoulder to the burden and submit to forced labor."*

Issachar wanted pleasantness and comfort. He realized that he could have comfort and convenience if he became a ... what? A slave. (Gen 49:14,15). This happened at the hands of the Assyrians. This was forced labor to pay a tax to the king of Assyria. There's that word, slavery again. She descended from a people who would accept slavery to have the pleasant land.

We have all come from Issachar.

We are the compromising tribe.

To get what we want, we become slaves.

For Reflection:

1. Find 3 areas of compromise in your life.

2. What motivates you to compromise? Is it fear, the love of comfort, or wanting your own way?

3. Do you have tendencies to use the things of God? This would include winning the praise or acceptance of others or compromise to have peace.

4. In what ways, do you identify with Gomer, with Hosea?

5. Can you identify areas of enslavement in your life? Ask the Lord to show you what He sees.

Prayer

Lord, help me understand what it means to be your betrothed. Help me see the purity and fidelity to which you call me. Draw me into your presence and transform my life.

You have purchased me from my harlot tendencies. I am your own. Make this truth real, so I will not view this from afar. Help me make it the air I breathe until I love and serve only you. Set me free from the slavery, I cannot recognize because I am so used to it. I do not see its insidious effects. Lord, you are the only one who helps me. You desire me, O glorious thought. Help me allow this to transform my life.

iv

Chapter 3

First Love

Better than Blessings

Song 1:2 "Let him kiss me with the kisses of his mouth - for your love is more delightful than wine."

Every story begins somewhere. This is the beginning of my story, yours too. Wine represents blessings in the Bible (Psa. 4:7, Jer.31:12). Remember when you first loved Him, how you yearned for Him more than any blessing. There was nothing you wanted more than Him. Back then, feeling that way was easy. Trials were few, and you had not learned how to "get things from God" yet. There was just Him. What happened to those days? In fact, slavery to others and compromise happened. Yet those were wonderful days while they lasted.

Song 1:3 "Pleasing is the fragrance of your perfumes; your name is like perfume poured out."

Remember the woman who poured perfume upon His feet just before His death? Since the perfume, He wears anointed Him for burial, even His name carries the fragrance of His sacrifice.

His death made you love Him more than any blessing. His sacrifice draws you to love Him that way again. The beginning, the center, and the end of this song are His death and all that included. Remember that. *His death was the most important event in all of history.* Without that, there would be no bride. Without His death, this song would be meaningless words on a page.

Perfume also speaks of the anointing oil and the incense used in the tabernacle and later in the temple. Because of her knowledge of this, she understands a bit about how precious His name is.

We will look at this in depth later. But for now, His name is as perfume or incense poured out.

Song 1:4 "Take me away with you - let us hurry! Let the king bring me into his chambers."

When did you last hurry to His chambers? Running out the door late for church doesn't count. These are His chambers, His innermost apartment, the Secret Place. This is the Holy of Holies, the presence of God's glory. These are chambers of the Bridegroom Lamb, the Lord of Lords.

Isn't it a shame? Slavery to sin and others keeps us so busy we do not have time to go there, and compromise so distracts us we do not notice. Or do we?

Perhaps that pain in your heart could be healed in His chambers. Oh, I see, you realize you hurt, but do not have the time to seek Him. Too busy working for the other masters? Do you remember when life was different?

Song 1:4b "We rejoice and delight in you, we praise your love more than wine." Do you remember when your friends viewed your life and your love for Him and loved Him too? They believed because of Him in you, His love was better than any blessing.

Song 1:4c "How right they are to adore you."

You knew it was right for others to desire Him as you did. Nothing was more important than He was. That was before you got so busy working in the church, so busy ministering for Him. That was before your own comfort became more important than being with Him, before you remembered there were so many people to please, impress, and whose love you wanted to win. You forgot for a season that others may reject you and that you fear failure. That was before you once again willingly submitted to slavery.

Sure, you complain about it.

But you made the choice.

Because slavery is what you know.

For Reflection:

1. Do you remember a time when you spent time with Him rather than do any other thing? How could you return to that devotion?

2. Are your friends inspired by your life today to know Him intimately, or do you inspire them to follow a belief system instead of Him?

3. Do you inspire anyone with your love of Him? If not, why not? How can you change this?

4. Do you rush to the Kings chambers? What keeps you from running to spend time with Him?

5. How are you serving things other than Him?

6. What priorities did you have when He was close? How can you regain those priorities or what does He want your present priorities to be?

Prayer

Lord, you have been so good. You love me so well you died to purchase me from slavery. Yet I barely see this truth.

I have forgotten much I knew at first. Life has intruded. But even more, I have allowed good things and my own desires to set you aside. Forgive me and restore the joy of my salvation. Help me love you, as I did at first. Set me free from the self-justification that says all is well. Show me what you see and call me to intimacy with you again. Help me. Only you can open my heart. Draw me so I might run into your presence and find everything I need in you.

Help me realize that everything I desire to see happen in my life can only come as I am in your presence and word. Lord, draw me to the place of intimacy in you. Set me free from the things that keep me from you and your transformational love.

FREEDOM IS OUR BIRTHRIGHT

Bride's Heart

Becoming The Bride Of Christ

5 STEPS TO A TRANSFORMED MIND

GAL. 5:1 FOR FREEDOM CHRIST HAS SET US FREE

Click the link or type into your search bar for your free book.

https://www.bridesheart.com/

Chapter 4

Mother's Sons

Sinful but Beautiful

Song 1:5 "Dark am I, yet lovely, O daughters of Jerusalem. Dark like the tents of Kedar, like the tent curtains of Solomon."

Remember the day when you saw the Slain Lamb and owned your sin. You realized you were black as the tents of black goatskins the nomads of Kedar use. You noticed because of Him you were lovely, like Solomon's royal tents. Those tents were white, interwoven with royal colors of blue and purple like the veil into the Holy of Holies. He is not only the one who made you lovely but also the one whose glory revealed your blackness, your sin and slavery to people and systems.

Song 1:6 "Do not stare at me because I am dark, because I am darkened by the sun,"

Feeling sorry for yourself, aren't you? You know you are lovely, but the rest of us can only see your darkness. In fact, we are skilled in staring at one another's blackness. This activity is part of slavery. If I stare at yours long enough, I will not notice how black I am. Then slavery will not hurt so much.

Song 1:6b "My mother's sons were angry with me and made me take care of the vineyards. My own vineyards I have neglected."

Cinderella

At last, we arrived at the passage that refers to slavery. This is the Bible Cinderella story. We know what caused Cinderella's sisters to persecute her, but why were the bride's brothers angry? What caused them to force her to labor for them? Jealousy and envy, the same problem Cinderella's sisters had. Jealousy is hostility toward someone who has something another person wants. Envy is worse than jealousy. Envy includes malice and a deep desire to see the person dispossessed of the coveted object, position, honor, or talent. Shulamite's brothers dispossessed her of her vineyard. Their vineyard thrived because, after all, they had her as their slave. Many churches, families, jobs friendships etc., are like this. Powerful people work to keep victims in a subordinate position. If one tries their own way in the church, job, relationship, or family, they must be made to bow to the powerful. Powerful people are jealous for their position. Thus, they must control (James 3:14-18).

Envy

How do we know the Mother's sons were jealous and envious of her? The context suggests it and since correct biblical interpretation uses scripture to interpret scripture, let us look at Joseph.

Genesis 37:3 'Now Israel loved Joseph more than any of his other sons, because he had born him in his old age; and he made a richly ornamented robe for him. When his brothers saw that their father loved him more than any of them, they hated him and could not speak a kind word to him.'

Joseph had a dream, and when he told it to his brothers, they hated him even more. Because he said to them, *"Listen to this dream I had: We were binding sheaves of grain out in the field* when suddenly my sheaf rose and stood upright, while your sheaves gathered around mine and bowed down to it."

'His brothers said to him, "Do you intend to reign over us? Do you intend to actually rule us?" And they hated him even more because of his dream and what he had said ' Older brothers own more power than younger brothers.

Likewise, envy and control are potent forces in families, jobs, relationships and churches. Even when envy is not a factor, control usually is. This causes wounds and strife in many lives. Control, domination, codependency, and game playing bring us into slavery.

Then he had another dream, and he told it to his brothers. "Listen," he said, "I had another dream and this time the sun and the moon and eleven stars were bowing down to me."

'When he told his father and his brothers, his father rebuked him and said, "What is this dream you had? Will your mother and I and your brothers actually come and bow down to the ground before you?" His brothers were jealous of him, but his father kept the matter in mind.'

Joseph's brothers were angry with him because of jealousy and envy due to the favoritism of their father. To make matters worse, Joseph had dreams showing him ruling over his brothers. When he told these dreams to his brothers, their anger and envy grew. His brothers dispossessed him of his father's love. They sold him as a slave. Did he deserve it? No, but he appeared black in their eyes. He boasted about his dreams, and they became angry. What they did was sinful however, his blackness justified their actions, they reasoned.

Whose Fault Is It?

That is confusing when slavery happens to you. Where does the slaveholder's sin end and yours begin? You will never know. Their sin is none of your business. However, your sin is very much your business.

In fact, I know they envied him because I experienced slavery and envy. Has it happened to you? If your answer is yes, you are in good company.

Joseph's brothers sold him as a slave.

Saul pursued David without cause, making him a fugitive (I Sam.18: 6-9, 19:10).

Cain killed Abel (Gen.4: 2-8).

The Pharisees crucified Jesus (Mark 15:10).

Scripture tells us that for envy, the Pharisees delivered Him up. Envy, power and control are very dangerous.

So is bitterness. You know the bitterness to which I refer. It is the bitterness living inside you against your mother's sons, against your slaveholders and persecutors.

When you learn to live out the Song of Songs, the bitterness will vanish. You will learn to rejoice in suffering. You will thank God for your Mother's sons because you will understand the purpose of the slavery.

That purpose makes it worthwhile.

I know.

I **was** bitter too.

Note "was bitter" is past tense.

Now I am grateful.

For example: when Jesus died envy against him ended. When Joseph exited the picture, envy ended. Sometimes it takes the death of the one envied for the Lord to redeem the situation. It was not fair for Jesus to be crucified or for Joseph to be sold into slavery. Through both God brought redemption.

Envy must dispossess so when it happens, embrace the Lord rather than blaming. Press into God instead of hating those who enslave you. He is the point. Slaves must learn to quit thinking like slaves, like victims. We must take responsibility for our own actions and our idolatries and fears because of being slaves. It is up to others to change their actions. We are the only ones who alter our own actions. We have the option to ask others around us or the Lord if there is anything we do that adds to the problem. If we do what we're supposed to, God might call us to give up our own desires. The New Testament calls it taking up our cross daily.

A few of us think that carrying the cross is only necessary on certain occasions or when we want to show off our spirituality. He calls us to lay our lives down for others daily. Jesus laid down His life and envy ended. He also took it up again. (Jn.10: 17-18) He told us no man took his life. He laid it down. Because of His example, we need to do the same for the sinners in our lives. And we must take our lives up again. Are you confused now?

We, like our Bridegroom, must listen to know when to lay our lives down. If we lay down our lives of our own choice because it is the will of God, then no one is taking it from us. Choice keeps us from being a victim. We are not accepting the terms of slavery they are offering, but are allowing His death to work in us. Whatever our time in the tomb, resurrection is the result. When we die, transformation results. This touches the world around us.

For Reflection

1. Have you been the object of envy? If you are not sure if it was envy, then perhaps persecution, or control, or slavery that brought significant loss to you.

2. How has envy, control, persecution, or loss affected your life?

3. What response did Jesus offer when He was envied, controlled, persecuted, suffered loss at the hands of others?

4. How is this different from your response?

5. How can you lay down your life in your current or future situations?

6. Think of the various people who hurt you in the past by enslaving you with control or dispossessed you. Will you forgive them? Write down their names. Pray for them until you sense no more frustration or negative emotions. Pray until you are free of them and receive God's heart for them. This could take hours, days, months, or years. Continue until all you wish for them is good.

Prayer

Father, there is so much pain. I feel as if my inner soul is obliterated. The pain engulfs my life, and I don't know how to get it resolved. Help me press into you, Lord. Help me recognize your glory is the point of everything. Show me how to release all of those who hurt me, even though in my mind they do not deserve it. Like me they deserve nothing but judgment. I will cry out to you for them and for my own heart until see them through your eyes instead of through my pain.

Help me, Lord, I cannot do this on my own. It is only through your strength this is possible. Help me then to know what position they should occupy in my life. Should I remain distant from them, or is there a chance for us to reconnect and fellowship once more? I give you my life, my heart, and my soul. They are yours; do with them, as you will. I surrender to you, the Lord of All.

Chapter 5

Slavery

Sold a Bill of Goods

If you are like most of us, you learned salvation means you experienced deliverance from Egypt and are freed from slavery forever. Though freedom is accomplished at salvation, the process takes a lifetime. Shulamite met the Bridegroom, but she was still a slave in her heart. Likewise, there are many people who love feeling important by enslaving others. They have a lot of practice and so have you. You are used to being a slave, not only a slave of others but also a slave of sin. Not yet able to count yourself dead to sin. Here's how it works.

Your slave tendencies from before salvation are still there. Redemption is progressing, but not finished. There are areas where the enemy can whisper in your ear, and each of these areas makes you vulnerable to slavery.

For example, do you fear man? Are you concerned about your reputation or the approval of others? That is all it takes to bring you in bondage to people.

Likewise, the word for fear, worship and awe are the word "yare" in the Hebrew. This means whatever you fear, you worship. If you fear the loss of money, you will ascribe awe or worship to money. Money will become your focus and you will become the ready slave of it. If you fear man or losing man's approval, you are ascribing awe or worship to men. Because of this, winning the approval of men will become your focus. You will serve men to earn their approval. If one's focus is on men or money, it is not on God. That which we fear losing becomes the object of worship. Fear of man (worship of man) gives men power over your life to victimize you. Worship of man brings slavery.

Think about the person who will help in any way at church. They are there more than anyone. Are they called to their endeavors, or do they worship the opinions of others? Do they serve so others will speak well of them. Or how about the person at work that stays for twelve or fourteen-hour days? Are they dealing with fear of man or fear of failure and worshipping success.

Another god we fear is money. The scriptures tell us we cannot serve God and money. If we try, we will love the one and hate the other. We cannot worship God and money at the same time. When we worship money, God becomes just one of the many gods to whom we bow. Similarly, the enemy, the ultimate slaveholder, convinces us we can serve other gods along with the Lord and not become slaves. We worship other gods and are blinded to it by deception. We do not realize we are enslaved.

If you fear man or rejection by man or losing the approval of the crowd, you have special radar that says, "Enslave me, victimize me." The slaveholders developed special radar too. You draw controllers to you since they have experience. They assure you they love you and only have your best interests at heart. They are your friend, boss, mate, shepherd etc. and say they care. Because you are naïve, you believe them.

Till one day

you wake up and realize

that you are actually

a slave.

I did.

Here is my story.

Slavery Begins

A significant family member during my growing-up years was always right. Always. Because of this, I was always wrong, always black. Though it is within the realm of possibility that this person admitted to being wrong, I do not remember it.

Being right is a terrible responsibility. There is a position to defend. One chief weapon of defence for the always right is anger. Growing up, I learned many lessons about anger. None was positive. Anger is often a tool to control and intimidate others. The victim/slave will do anything to avoid outbursts. Victims can never do enough.

There is another alternative, fight back. Then the victim becomes angry too. Some victims alternately lay down under persecution or get angry. They aren't sure whether to be an angry persecutor, or a defeated victim. Every angry persecutor was once a defeated victim who dealt with the pain by learning to control. The slave becomes the persecutor. In fact, this brings spiritual slavery and not a way to freedom.

The victim has a problem with fear and so does the persecutor. Persecutors are the most fearful people on the planet. Persecutors dictate because they are afraid someone will overthrow their position of power. This is true even though they seem so self-assured. The self-assurance is a smokescreen to hide the persecutor's pain. In fact, fear is so well hidden that often the persecutor does not realize it exists. Fear is the reason they persecute. They must control their sphere. They do not realize their kingdom is established on intimidation, fuelled by their own fear.

Coming to love Christ, I thought everything would change. Others told me so. With salvation God, would wave His magic wand and the problems of the past would disappear. That piece of misinformation is a weapon in the enemies' arsenal to ensnare and discourage the saints. Did I get ensnared? I sure did.

I became the slave of many that claimed to have authority in the church. Submission was important and the fellowship of the God's people. Commitment to both was imperative. Likewise, I feared other's disapproval. This means I worshipped their approval and ascribed awe to them that belongs only to God.

There are people in the church looking for people like me. I wanted authority figures to love me even if they felt I was wrong, healing the past pain. Since slaveholders cannot love those who are wrong, they use that situation to bring further bondage upon the slave. After all, the slave was wrong; they need more control, not less.

I also wanted to be right, for once in my life, instead of wrong, wrong, wrong. Inside, I believed if I were right, they would love me. Slaveholders are faultless, at least in their own minds. Thus, you cannot win when you are a slave. There is only one opinion of events allowed that of the slave master. There is no way to be right.

The worst slavery existed in my mind. I had come out of Egypt, but in my soul, I was still a slave, a hopeless, worthless slave, a tormented soul. Remember the voices of Chapter 1. Voices to the right and left kept speaking. Those were the voices of people in my present circumstances, telling me how wrong I was again. The voice behind me spoke. That voice of the past and a significant family member gave power to the other voices. Because of my past, I knew nothing would ever change.

I became utterly.

hopeless.

There are other points we need to understand about slavery before we can learn its purpose or experience healing from torment. These next things are only implied in the text, but if you ask any slave, he will say this happens.

Shulamite's brothers forced her to bring forth fruit for them in their garden, then told her, "You have no fruit." In fact, they neglected to mention she had no time to keep her own vineyard since she was keeping theirs.

Has this been said to you? Don't take it to heart. Slaveholders do not know their slaves anyhow. slaveholders use them, but they don't know them. They stay distant and what looks like leaves from 200 feet away could be full of apples up close. They never got close enough to the tree to see the fruit.

Shame and Fear

They force her to stay in the sun, then they laugh at her blackness. She is ashamed of the blackness, but the wounds that keep her a slave cause her blackness. For example: The Lord showed me in picture form what this is like.

I was standing naked and in need of a bath. Authority told me I may not have a bath in the big claw-foot tub in front of me. They forced me to take a bath in a small modern sink.

As I sat in the tiny bowl of the sink, the only thing that fit was my posterior. I could not get clean. I had no choice but to sit there naked, exposed, and dirty. Then authority paraded people past me to show them my blackness and dirt.

I knew I was dirty. I wanted to be clean, but they denied me the means to bathe. Then the parade of people saw my dirt.

Thus, slaveholders cannot see the bride's heart. They are too busy criticizing her behind her back to dispossess her of the respect of the group. They cannot see her beauty, only the blackness for which they share responsibility. However, she gets a glimpse of His beauty in her. She sees herself as dark because of the slavery but lovely because the Bridegroom's love makes her lovely.

She only knows this when she gets her focus off her mother's sons, her slaveholders. In fact, if she keeps her focus on them, she will end up bitter. If they fill her vision, she cannot see the Lord. Only in seeing Him will she know she is not only black but also lovely.

Only in seeing Him

will she have the courage

to stop being a slave.

For Reflection:
1. How are you a slave of sin? (Romans 7)
2. How were the Israelites still slaves?

Ex. 14:11 They said to Moses, "Was it because there were no graves in Egypt that you brought us to the desert to die? What have you done to us by bringing us out of Egypt?

Ex. 14:12 Didn't we say to you in Egypt, 'Leave us alone; let us serve the Egyptians'? It would have been better for us to serve the Egyptians than to die in the desert!"

Ex. 17:3But the people were thirsty for water there, and they grumbled against Moses. They said, "Why did you bring us up out of Egypt to make us and our children and livestock die of thirst?"

Num. 21:5 they spoke against God and against Moses, and said, "Why have you brought us up out of Egypt to die in the desert? There is no bread! There is no water! And we detest this miserable food!"

3. How are you a slave of others?

4. How does your heart betray you? How did the hearts of the Israelites betray them? Heb. 3, Heb. 12:3-5, Acts 28:27, Lu. 12:29-34, Lu. 10:27

5. What lie makes you submit to slavery? What did the enemy whisper to Eve, and what was the result? (Genesis Gen. 3:1-19) How does fear play into this?

6. Identify 5 fears you see active in your life. What fears did the Israelites have? (Ex. 14:10, Ex 19-Ex 20)

7. What part does unbelief (lack of trust) play in fear? (Heb. 3)

9. What scriptures can help you overcome this? Ask the Lord to show you where to stand in His word.

10. Are there any people you bring in bondage to you? Who attempts to bring you into bondage?

11. Ask the Lord to show you what step you must take so you can become free of bringing others into bondage? How can you quit submitting to others who desire to enslave you?

13. Has someone (and your own idolatry) forced you to work as a slave and then had them criticize your "blackness"? Ask the Lord what to do to prevent this. Let Him show you any dynamic in your life that invites this.

14. Since wounded-ness helps keeps us slaves, and that causes our blackness, how can we get free? (Song 4:7, James 4:7-8, Psalm 45 10-17, Jere. 29:11-12, Jere. 30:17)

15. What kind of focus will help you overcome the effects of this in your life?

Gal. 1:10 For am I now seeking the favor of men, or of God? Or am I striving to please men? If I were still trying to please men, I would not be a bondservant of Christ." Paul was a slave (bond servant is literally slave) of Christ. This set him free of man pleasing.

Gal. 2:20 "I have been crucified with Christ; and it is no longer I who live, but Christ lives in me; and the life which I now live in the flesh I live by faith in the Son of God, who loved me and gave Himself up for me."

Ask the Lord to show you what it means for you to be crucified with Him. Write this down. Memorize this scripture and let it guide your future. Embrace your cross and if you struggle with this, ask the Lord's help. Determine to die to everything that holds your heart but Him. Cry out for Him to show you other scriptures that will help you leave slavery behind.

Prayer

Lord, help me quit surrendering to slavery. Heal my soul, so I am completely yours. I cannot see many areas of my life. I only see the sinful behaviours that result from those broken areas and attitudes. Reveal how and why sin enslaves me and set me free from the things that fight against your glory expressed through my life. I surrender to you anew for I have no power to bring cause this. I only have you. Sometimes I am overwhelmed with confusion and cannot see a way out. Show me the way. Open the scriptures so I can stop serving as a slave to people and become yours.

Help me embrace your cross. I am so broken that it seems this would only bring more pain. How can more suffering be the road to freedom? This is a question that rings within me. But I choose you. I choose your cross. I choose my cross. Work in me the truth that I have been crucified with Christ and I no longer live. Help me exchange slavery to people for being a slave of Christ. Help me realize that the devotion required brings me into an intimate relationship with you.

I desire that, but it feels sometimes so far off as to be a dream. I choose trust in your word and your heart. You will bring me to that place of intimate fellowship. You are the only one who can. Help me choose you repeatedly and learn to trust you with my entire being.

Chapter 6

Forget the Past

A Long Journey

This slavery passage we looked at only took up two verses out of eight chapters of Song of Songs. So, slavery must be of short duration. Wrong! God declared emancipation. We need to act on it. Unless we become free of the past, we stay slaves.

To forget the past, we must first see through God's eyes what the past has done to us. We must identify the idols the past has taught us to worship. Then wrestle with our broken soul and behaviors that come out of it. Thus, forgetting the past is imperative to the readiness of the bride for the Bridegroom.

Have you ever sensed that you are a slave to sin? Have you ever found yourself taken advantage of, enslaved to others, abused? Do you enslave and abuse others? The Israelites came out of slavery in Egypt, yet in the wilderness they still behave like slaves. In Ex. 15-17 the people complain of thirst and hunger and the need for meat. Hebrews 3-4 says they tested the Lord because of their unbelief. These are the same people the Lord brought out of Egypt by opening the Red Sea and closing it again on Pharaoh and his army, destroying them. We are the people released from slavery by believing Jesus died to save us from our sin. The enemy's power to hunt us down and take us back to slavery is destroyed. However, we often act as if the slaveholders still have power.

For example, we struggle with unbelief as they did. We hear God's promise to us and often live as if He never made a promise. He shows us what He wants us to do, and we choose other directions. We struggle with fear of poverty, fear of others hurting us, fear of judgment, fear of rejection, fear of man and other fears ad infinitum. We do this because we are slaves of fear, unbelief, and behaviors ingrained in our personality.

Similarly, we struggle with slavery to sin until the day we die. Discovering freedom from the control of others is possible, but it's only through a lifetime of applying the cross that the Lord liberates us from self-imposed bondage.

Rom. 7:21 "So I find this law at work: When I want to do good, evil is right there with me.

Rom. 7:22 For in my inner being I delight in God's law;

Rom. 7:23 but I see another law at work in the members of my body, waging war against the law of my mind and making me a prisoner of the law of sin at work within my members.

Rom. 7:24 What a wretched man I am! Who will rescue me from this body of death?

Rom. 7:25 Thanks be to God—through Jesus Christ our Lord! So then, I myself in my mind am a slave to God's law, but in the sinful nature, a slave to the law of sin.

Rom. 8:1 Therefore, there is now no condemnation for those who are in Christ Jesus,"

We daily fight against the enslavement of our enemy. Any victory we enjoy is made possible only through the sacrifice of our Lord Jesus Christ, our Bridegroom Lamb. And though we struggle daily, there is no condemnation for those in Christ. However, we often feel guilty and condemned. On days when we are honest, we notice our idolatry and it appalls us.

Until we come to Christ, we are slaves. Until we are whole inside and free of others and the lies of the enemy, we stay slaves. Some people are slaves for life. They cannot conceive of life apart from slavery. Rather, the next steps of relationship with the Bridegroom are something to which they cannot commit. They are saved; they love him, but they are not free. Our Bridegroom wants to take us on the path to freedom, but our cost is great. It is the cost of passion. Passion has a price. His passion for us cost Him everything. Similarly, our passion for Him should do no less. Passion means we seek Him to know Him more than anything this world offers. It means we will pay any cost for this one consuming passion. When we cannot see the way ahead, and the past and the voice of fear given power by that past are screaming out that there is no hope, we hold on to the One who holds us even when we cannot feel Him.

How do we leave slavery behind with its intendant hurt? What is the strategy to liberate ourselves from the slavery of our past mistakes and hurts? Is there a way to detect behaviors, and the hidden false identities that drive them?

False Beliefs

For example, do you interpret passion for service and notoriety as passion for Him? Do you believe you have paid the price for ministry? But have you paid the price for passion for Him? Is the price you paid because of the deception or the behaviors in your life? There is a difference.

Similarly, if you pursue service on your own terms, you may fulfil your need for acceptance or fame rather than the will of God. Is your ministry/service done for others to see or to delight His heart? Does your ministry make you look good or bring Him glory? Even fleshly ministry/service will have "nay-Sayers" and appear to have a cost. This is the cost of doing business, not the cost of passion. Likewise, are you paying normal business costs or paying the price to know Him as He IS rather than knowing Him through your fears and idolatries?

We are called to minister to someone. The more difficult the call, often the greater will be the wounding, sacrifice, and misunderstanding. The reward on the surface will be only greater passion, which itself invites greater wounding, sacrifice, and misunderstanding from those who want ease. There is another benefit, however, more of Him. If you know His heart's passion, you know Him.

Are you content to leave ministry to paid clergy? Are you willing to search for a comfortable spiritual life that costs you little? The most amazing thing about this is that the Church is His plan A. He has NO plan B. Because of this, His passion is to move through His Church to reach the world. He sees us as a bride who is perfect through His blood, and we ravish His heart.

Do you know what breaks His heart? How about what brings Him joy? Have you understood that righteousness and justice are the foundation of His throne, the foundation of His rule and reign in your life? Does your heart ache because of it? Does your heart rejoice because of it?

Do you have a thorough understanding of what it means to be His bride? Is your heart committed to fidelity to Him alone? Have you allowed Him to illuminate your inner temple and reveal the idols within you? Have you let Him drive the "money changers" from your heart? Are you ready for the wedding supper of the Lamb? Do you value life lived in His presence more than anything life offers? Do you ache to have time alone with Him?

We could ask a thousand more questions. To every question, our best answer is, "I have set my heart toward Him." To many of the questions, we could not go that far. Instead, we will come back with an entire list of questions such as "how do we get ready for Him? How do we pay the price for passion? What does it mean to lose everything for Him? "Why do we have to lose more when we have lost so much already? Are you kidding? I poured my heart and soul into serving Him, only to be met with more suffering and perplexity. Song of Songs shows us the way to God.

Getting Ready

Rev. 19:7   "Let us rejoice and be glad
and give him glory!
For the wedding of the Lamb has come,
and his bride has made herself ready.
Rev. 19:8   Fine linen, bright and clean,
was given her to wear."
(Fine linen stands for the righteous acts of the saints.)
Rev. 19:9 Then the angel said to me, "Write: 'Blessed are those who are invited to the wedding supper of the Lamb!'" And he added, "These are the true words of God."

Note that in the passage above, *"His bride has made herself ready. Fine linen, bright and clean, was given her to wear. 'Fine linen stands for the righteous acts of the saints'"*. We receive our bridal garments from Him. They become ours when we perform righteous acts. For example: is it a righteous act to build a ministry to our own glory? Is it a righteous act to work hard at church work so people will tell us how wonderful we are? What righteous acts do we need to perform? *Rev 19:7a "and give him glory!* We should live our lives for His glory, not our own. Are we living to know His heart and then bringing others to know His heart also? Are we willing to pay the price to know His heart? Will we let go of the other gods we worship in America and around the world? Will we give up the gods of comfort and convenience, praise of men, superstar religious leader, whining, self-pity, victimology, and greed, to name a few?

One of our difficulties is the behaviors and identity that come out of our wounded-ness. They are so much a part of our lives we think we **are** those behaviors. We do not understand who He is making us to be. We are locked in a struggle that feels like we will never rise above. However, when we reach man-made goals, we think we have arrived. Despite this He looks forward to our fullness as we see in Revelation 21.

Rev. 21:2 "I saw the Holy City, the new Jerusalem, coming down out of heaven from God, prepared as a bride beautifully dressed for her husband."

Rev. 21:9 "One of the seven angels who had the seven bowls full of the seven last plagues came and said to me, "Come, I will show you the bride, the wife of the Lamb."

Rev. 21:10 "And he carried me away in the Spirit to a mountain great and high, and showed me the Holy City, Jerusalem, coming down out of heaven from God."

If we are called to Him, we are to be prepared as the wife of the Lamb. This means the wife of the one who died for us. He sees us as beautiful, and; thus, He is getting us ready for our wedding day at the culmination of all things.

However, we are not called to ease or comfort. He calls us to Him the Lamb of God. We must know His heart for the world, poor, dying and "the least of these". What makes Him cry? What breaks His heart? He is remaking us to be concerned with His heart's desires and building His Kingdom. He is calling us to see through His eyes.

For example: we were called out 50 years ago, when Martin Luther King Jr. wrote that we would see what people are made of when they face difficulty. Not when all is going well. Comfort and convenience do not reveal the authentic person. This was 5 years before his assassination for the cause so near to the heart of God, he felt compelled by his knowledge of God's heart to fulfil the call. To do less would have been unthinkable. Serving the gods of comfort and convenience was not his way. He embraced difficulty for the sake of the heart of this nation, his people, and his Lord. That difficulty took his life and helped to grow the equal rights movement into a juggernaut that changed the culture and continues to change the culture of the USA until this day.

Martin Luther King Jr. marched against the injustice of slavery. Where are the intercessors that cry out against the bondage that keeps the Church from her inheritance in the Kingdom?

If the Lord were here today to which Church institutions, would He say, "woe Pharisees"? How did the church's Phariseeism contribute to the lack of rights for black America? How does it contribute to the racial divide in our churches and our lack of concern for others today? We are to get ready for the Bridegroom. We are far from ready. See what happens to those who call us to the wedding supper.

His Messengers

Throughout the years, the Lord sent out messengers to invite the Church to the wedding supper. The Lamb of God, in Matt. 22, documents their reception by most of the Church.

Matt. 22:1 "Jesus spoke to them again in parables, saying: Matt. 22:2 "The kingdom of heaven is like a king who prepared a wedding banquet for his son."

Matt. 22:3 "He sent his servants to those who had been invited to the banquet to tell them to come, but they refused to come."

Matt. 22:4 "Then he sent some more servants and said, 'Tell those who have been invited that I have prepared my dinner: My oxen and fattened cattle have been butchered, and everything is ready. Come to the wedding banquet.'

Matt. 22:5 "But they paid no attention and went off—one to his field, another to his business."

Most of the Church and similarly before them, the nation of Israel solved the problem of these messengers by ignoring them.

The American Church is too busy with jobs and pursuing the American Dream. Too busy with the idols we serve along with serving the Lord. Rather, we are segregated in our enclaves, busy with "church" and missing those He will invite.

Matt. 22:6 "The rest seized his servants, mistreated them and killed them."

Others mistreated them and sometimes brutalized them, so the servants retreated from ministry. They needed time to heal. Others, like Martin Luther King Jr. lost their lives for God's cause.

Matt. 22:7 "The king was enraged. He sent his army and destroyed those murderers and burned their city."

A day is coming when the Lord will judge the strongholds that harmed the messengers He sent. The strongholds that caused this problem will face destruction and burning. The King of Love is angry for that which harmed His bride. Thus, when He wipes out the strongholds of hate, selfishness, harlotry, busyness, comfort, convenience, prejudice, fear and so forth, we need to recognize them as enemies rather than friends. May the smoke of their burning rise before Him and us, reminding us He alone is God.

Matt. 22:8 "Then he said to his servants, 'The wedding banquet is ready, but those I invited did not deserve to come.

Matt. 22:9 Go to the street corners and invite to the banquet anyone you find."

Thus, the messengers sent out in recent history hid in mega churches and out of the way places, so they could heal. Now they have received a new mandate to go to the street corners and "invite anyone you find". This time, His servants will not go primarily to the Church. They will bring everyone they find. Through them God will mentor a younger generation to invite others.

Matt. 22:10 So the servants went out into the streets and gathered all the people they could find, both good and bad, and the wedding hall was filled with guests.

Matt. 22:11 "But when the king came in to see the guests, he noticed a man there who was not wearing wedding clothes.

Matt. 22:12 'Friend,' he asked, 'how did you get in here without wedding clothes?' The man was speechless.

Matt. 22:13 "Then the king told the attendants, 'Tie him hand and foot, and throw him outside, into the darkness, where there will be weeping and gnashing of teeth.'

The Lord will invite everyone to come. Yet not all who come to the banquet will receive the wedding clothes He provides. But "the bride has made herself ready." The servants are to invite, but they cannot qualify who is ready. That is His job.

The Pretender

The man thrown out was a pretender. It's possible that he believed his actions were enough to qualify him for being there. Similarly, we are told that our righteousness must exceed that of the Pharisees. The Pharisees had a set of rules they thought will satisfy God. A set of rules without relationship with Him is not our calling. The bride makes herself ready in intimate communion with the one who called her. Intimacy is the hallmark of genuine relationship.

The Church is worldly, idolatrous, but within her are a people who will reach the world.

Ezekiel the prophet was an Israelite who was taken captive by the Babylonians and removed to Babylon. He prophesied while living in Babylon of the coming invasion and destruction of Jerusalem and the temple. Jeremiah and Isaiah warned the nation of Judah for years before the captivity. The first group of captives taken to Babylon was a second warning. However, the nation's leaders did not heed the warning.

Let us look at the temple of Ezekiel's day to understand the symbolism of our relationship with God.

Temple Design

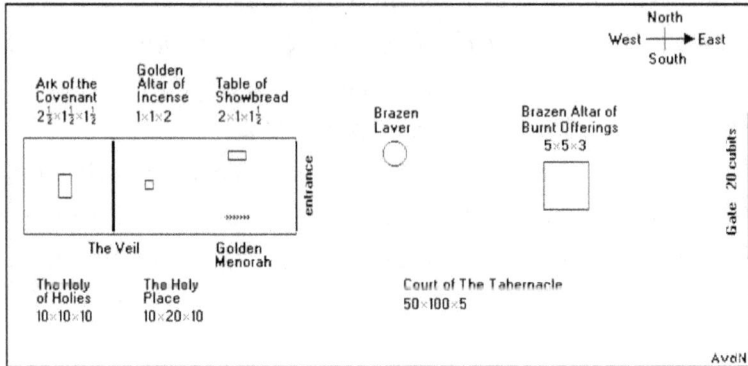

The temple included an Outer Court or the court of the gentiles. Even the stranger could come this far. Many who attend our churches come only this far.

The next chamber is the Inner Court. This chamber had two pieces of furniture. There was an altar where the sacrifices for sin took place. This is a type of the death of the Lamb of God. The priest placed his hand on the animal's head, signifying the transfer of sins to the animal. Then the priests killed the animal. There was a laver, which was a large bath for washing. This is a type of us being washed of our sin. Likewise, many others who attend church come only this far.

Two chambers made up the next part of the temple. The first chamber was the Holy Place. The only person allowed to enter was the priest. There were three items in the Holy Place. Inside was a table of showbread, a type of the word of God and Jesus, the bread of life. There was a candlestick (menorah), a type of the work of the Holy Spirit. Both the oil of the lamp and its light speak of the Holy Spirit's anointing and the illumination the Spirit brings to the word. The last piece of furniture was an incense altar. The incense altar is a type of prayer and worship being lifted to God. This is a type of intimate communion with the Holiest of All.

Unless he took incense from this altar, the priest could not enter the next chamber. Believers study the word and let God's light in. But there is a further step.

The next chamber is the Holy of Holies. The words Holy of Holies show that there is nothing holier. Once a year, the High Priest entered the Holy of Holies to make atonement for the people. He must come into it in the prescribed way or God will strike him dead. Priests tied a rope to his ankle in case that happened. Then they could drag out his dead body. The Holy of Holies is where God dwelled with His people by His Glory. God would not strike the priest dead because He is vengeful, but He is so holy that only that which is holy stands in His presence without suffering this fate. Thus, the Holy of Holies is the step into intimacy, into the bridal chamber today. We hang back because we are afraid of what needs to die. We fear the suffering.

The priest had to go around a thick curtain to get into the Holy of Holies. There was no middle opening. When Jesus died, we are told:

Matt. 27:51 At that moment, the curtain of the temple was torn in two from top to bottom. The earth shook and the rocks split.

This curtain kept people out of the Holy of Holies and kept unclean worshippers from being struck dead. When Jesus died, the hand of God tore this curtain in two from top to bottom. The death of Jesus gave us free access to God's presence. This means we may go into the presence of the One who is Totally Other. His glory has the power to kill a man, yet we have free access. He is the one who resides in us.

Heb.10:19 Therefore, brothers, since we have confidence to enter the Most Holy Place by the blood of Jesus,

Heb. 10:20 by a new and living way opened for us through the curtain, that is, his body,

We are God's temple, so there is much we learn by a look at the temple of Ezekiel's day. The following narrative is what God revealed to Ezekiel about His view of the temple.

The Glory of God manifests His presence. Jesus was the Glory and His torn human body was also the curtain. See the example of what happens to the Glory of God below, as shown to Ezekiel when he was captive in Babylon.

Ezek. 8:3 "He stretched out what looked like a hand and took me by the hair of my head. The Spirit lifted me up between earth and heaven and in visions of God, he took me to Jerusalem, to the entrance to the north gate of the inner court, where the idol that provokes to jealousy stood.

Ezek. 8:4 "And there before me was the glory of the God of Israel, as in the vision I had seen in the plain.

Ezek. 8:5 Then he said to me, Son of man, look toward the north. So, I looked, and in the entrance north of the gate of the altar I saw this idol of jealousy."

This is the temple with God's glory. The Glory normally occupies the Holy of Holies. The Glory is instead in the inner court. In this temple, north of the altar, was an idol that provoked the Lord to jealousy. Because of this, the Glory was prepared to leave the temple.

The Captive God

The Jews of that day believed that God occupied the Holy of Holies and would not leave. Their belief convinced them they had God captive in the Holy of Holies. Because they had Him captive, they need not fear invasion or judgment, no matter what they did to break the covenant, no matter how many idols they brought into His temple. Similarly, this is a picture of today's Church.

Ezek. 8:9"And he said to me, "Go in and see the wicked and detestable things they are doing here."

Ezek. 8:10 So I went in and looked, and I saw portrayed all over the walls all kinds of crawling things and detestable animals and all the idols of the house of Israel. "

When we come to Christ, we become His temple. There are idols of greed, selfishness, mammon, hatred, apathy etc. inscribed on the walls of our hearts. The process of salvation is to set us free from them if we will allow it. The Israelites of Ezekiel's day did not allow it. They kept bringing more and more idols into the temple. Whenever you read the word idolatry, you could substitute slavery in its place. Whatever we behold reverently, we serve. We either become slaves of God or slaves of the enemy. Likewise, we are like the people of Ezekiel's day, since deception blinds us to our slavery/idolatry. The nature of deception is that you do not realize you are deceived.

Ezek. 8:11 In front of them stood seventy elders of the house of Israel, and Jaazaniah son of Shaphan was standing among them. Each had a censer in his hand, and a fragrant cloud of incense was rising.

Ezek. 8:12 He said to me, "Son of man, have you seen what the elders of the house of Israel are doing in the darkness, each at the shrine of his own idol? They say, 'The LORD does not see us; the LORD has forsaken the land.'"

Each one of us looks like Ezekiel's temple whenever we give our lives to Jesus. We must recognize this and seek the Lord for freedom from the things that hold our hearts from the idols inscribed on our walls. God's people in this passage believed that He had forsaken them. When trouble comes, we feel forsaken. Fear motivated idolatry then and now. The elders of Israel were afraid that they would not have rain and crops, so they prayed to other gods. They sacrificed their children to other gods because of fear. Thus, they entertained other gods whom they believed could do more for them. We also move in fear and try to make everything come out alright. We worship money and jobs, greed and avarice, and call it God's will. The other gods are so much a part of our daily lives and culture, even the Church culture, that we do not recognize them as idols.

Leaders were worshipping idols out of fear. "Each at the shrine of his own idol" Likewise, any leaders and members of the Body of Christ are still doing this today.

For Reflection

1. What lies do you believe that make you a slave?
2. What do you need to give up, making Him your passion?
3. Are you willing to commit to whatever it takes for Him to set you free?
4. What idols are inside your temple? Ask Him to show you what they are. Ask Him to help you forsake all your other lovers.
5. Do you have a thorough understanding of what it means to be His bride? Listen to Him about what the next step is for you.

Prayer

Lord, I have so many passions, so many idols. I did not realize how many until now. Forgive me and help me get free. I don't want to continue to serve other gods. I do not see the fear accurately. Only you have the power set me free from the fear that allows the other gods to reign in me. Show me the road to freedom. Draw me into the Your presence. Live in and through me, Lord of All.

Chapter 7

Idols Lies and the Road to Freedom

Only One Weapon

The enemy of our souls has only one weapon. That is the lie. If he gets us to believe his lies, then he keeps us slaves. Slavery is how God deals in our lives to set us free from the lie if we will let Him. But first we must become sick of slavery and perhaps even beyond hope that an answer to our dilemma exists.

So, what are the lies? The lies are part of the cost. To us, they don't appear as lies but as truth. That is the problem. The lies have been a part of us so long we guide our lives by them. They make us miserable, but they are the only reality we know. We are reluctant to part with them. We fight the pain of the process that makes us free.

One big lie is, "You are worthless." The person who lives considering this rejects all proof to the contrary. Then the lie says, "God does not really love you. He sits in heaven with a baseball bat and cracks you over the head every time you step out of line." Those who believe God is like this, find leaders, friends or mates that are like this and become their willing slave. When these others hurt them, it proves that the lie they believe is true. This is good news/bad news. This confirms reality they live by, but they are wounded again. Consolation is scarce. They find it impossible to come near to God consistently if this lie is alive in them.

"You must perform to be loved," is another colossal lie. Workaholics, people who feel driven to accomplish, serve, help and minister, struggle with this. That is most of us. This lie causes most of the stress we endure. Performance motivated people believe they must perform not only for others but, for God. They often take on responsibility, not theirs, and live in a world of "have to", "should have" and "what if". Condemnation is their daily food. The way they overcome condemnation is to do more, perform more, and please people more to keep condemnation at bay. Fear of not performing well is their daily food. This makes it simple to shift from a balanced view of scripture to legalism. Since most of the church is performance based, this represents a big problem.

The enemy's main purpose for lies is to cause fear. If we fear, we become slaves to the things we fear losing. In the scriptures, the word that we translate fear is also translated awe and worship. Whatever we fear, we worship, worship that belongs only to God. When we feel worthless, we fear having it proven to us by rejection. Then we worship others' good opinions of us. If we believe God has a baseball bat for us, we have an unhealthy fear of God that does not receive the balance of His grace. If we must perform to be loved because of fear of rejection, we can never do enough. There is a cycle of perform-condemnation, perform-condemnation.

A New Word

The entire process of slavery makes us disgusted and angry enough to question the reality by which we guide our lives. Only when we become hopeless or cannot go on are we finally ready to hear the truth.

We are living out of an old dynamic. It is an old word from our old father (the devil). Thus, we need to receive a new word from our new Father (God). How do we do this?

This is simple, but it's difficult. We must replace the old word with a new word. This means we do not look at the "apparent" evidence before us, the circumstances. We do not regard other voices. We listen only to One voice. The old voices are very loud, making this difficult. We will look at this in-depth later.

What self-created idols keep you from intimacy? Do people's opinions or your desire for power and respect keep you from him? Let us look at the Israelites idols.

Ezek. 8:14 "Then he brought me to the entrance to the north gate of the house of the LORD, and I saw women sitting there, mourning for Tammuz.

Ezek. 8:15 He said to me, "Do you see this, son of man? You will see things that are even more detestable than this.

Ezek. 8:16 He then brought me into the inner court of the house of the LORD, and there, at the entrance to the temple, between the portico and the altar, were about twenty-five men. With their backs toward the temple of the LORD and their faces toward the east, they were bowing down to the sun in the east."

Ezek. 9:3 "Now the glory of the God of Israel went up from above the cherubim, where it had been, and moved to the threshold of the temple. Then the LORD called to the man clothed in linen who had the writing kit at his side. Ezek. 9:4 and said to him, "Go throughout the city of Jerusalem and put a mark on the foreheads of those who grieve and lament over all the detestable things that are done in it. Ezek. 10:4 Then the glory of the LORD rose from above the cherubim and moved to the threshold of the temple. The cloud filled the temple, and the court was full of the radiance of the glory of the LORD."

The leaders in the Lord's earthly temple had power and respect. They used it to lead the people into worship. The problem was they were worshipping idols and thought that was acceptable to God. They led God's people astray.

Because of the idolatry, the angel marks the foreheads of those who grieve over the sin. This is like the last days. So, do you grieve and lament over your sin and the sin of the church? Do you realize our nation is in trouble and the church is at fault? Since the church resembles the world, like American culture, it is irrelevant to most people. The church is responsible for the cultural deterioration in our nation.

In this passage, the Glory is leaving the temple. It is by the threshold instead of in the Holy of Holies. When the Glory leaves, the Babylonians will destroy the temple, and the Israelites taken captive to Babylon.

Ezek. 10:18 "Then the glory of the LORD departed from over the threshold of the temple and stopped above the cherubim."

Ezek. 10:19 "While I watched, the cherubim spread their wings and rose from the ground, and as they went, the wheels went with them. They stopped at the entrance to the east gate of the LORD'S house, and the glory of the God of Israel was above them."

The Glory Leaves

Ezek. 11:23 "The glory of the LORD went up from within the city and stopped above the mountain east of it."

The glory stopped at the Mount of Olives. Jewish tradition says Jeremiah sat on the Mount of Olives as he watched the temple burn and wrote the book of Lamentations.

Watch what happens when Jesus ministered. Jesus is ready to leave the temple for the last time.

Matt. 23:29 '" Woe to you, teachers of the law and Pharisees, you hypocrites! You build tombs for the prophets and decorate the graves of the righteous.

Matt. 23:30 And you say, 'If we had lived in the days of our forefathers, we would not have taken part with them in shedding the blood of the prophets.'

Matt. 23:31 So you testify against yourselves that you are the descendants of those who murdered the prophets.

Matt. 23:32 Fill up, then, the measure of the sin of your forefathers!

Matt. 23:33 You snakes! You brood of vipers! How will you escape being condemned to hell?

Matt. 23:34 Therefore I am sending you prophets and wise men and teachers. Some of them you will kill and crucify; others you will flog in your synagogues and pursue from town to town.

Matt. 23:35 And so upon you will come all the righteous blood that has been shed on earth, from the blood of righteous Abel to the blood of Zechariah, son of Berekiah, whom you murdered between the temple and the altar.

Matt. 23:36 I tell you the truth, all this will come upon this generation."'

The leaders of Jesus' day thought they were better than their fathers. Unlike their fathers, they will recognize those God sent to them, especially Messiah. Yet they did not recognize Jesus. Many today do not recognize those He has sent. In this passage, Jesus is mourning over the blindness of the church leaders. A few days after speaking the words in this passage, they crucified Him.

Matt. 23:37 "O Jerusalem, Jerusalem, you who kill the prophets and stone those sent to you, how often I have longed to gather your children together, as a hen gathers her chicks under her wings, but you were not willing.

Matt. 23:38 Look, your house is left to you desolate.

Matt. 23:39 For I tell you, you will not see me again until you say, 'Blessed is he who comes in the name of the Lord.'"

*Matt. 24: "**Jesus left the temple and was walking away** (emphasis mine) when his disciples came up to him to call his attention to its buildings.*

Matt. 24:2 Do you see all these things? He asked. "I tell you the truth, not one stone here will be left on another; everyone will be thrown down."

*Matt. 24:3 As **Jesus was sitting on the Mount of Olives**,"* (emphasis mine).

The Mount of Olives

The Glory of God (Jesus) left the physical temple for the last time and sat on the Mount of Olives just as the Glory left the temple in Ezekiel's day. Ezekiel 8-11. Construction of Herod's temple was finished in 65 A.D. In 70 AD, an army destroyed the temple and Jesus' words as His Glory left the temple were fulfilled.

What happened in Ezekiel's, Jeremiah's and Isaiah's time happens again, only this time they refused God in the flesh. If He comes to His temple, He has the option to leave His temple. Thus, we cannot keep Him captive in our church, temple, or in the box we have constructed.

When the Lord dealt with the idols, I constructed He took from me the many behaviors I used to control the outcomes of my life. Many idols He is pursuing in our lives are in the next paragraphs.

Rationalization is a psychological word that describes seduction and deception. Humas suffer from self-seduction and self-deception. There are different levels, but everyone is self-deceived.

Self-seduction and self-deception keep us from seeing our most hidden motives. Before we are self-deceived, we are self-seduced. We rationalize our behavior and our propensity to control life to get our own way. Then we control others and the outcomes of life.

When we come to Christ, we still do this to others, controlling them by our actions. As we walk with Him and He purifies us through the fire, we no longer want to control others. But the seduction and deception of self still lives in our mind, keeping us from seeing one of the most important truths we need to be free. We want to control our destiny. Further, this means we are controlling God. We believe His presence is captive.

Self-deception and self-seduction keep us from seeing this futile form of control. If we serve a god, we control He is not the God Who IS. If we are motivated by fear of anything other than the Lord, we are at some level controlling our destiny or attempting to control God.

Controlling God is an oxymoron, impossible and a dunderheaded thing to do. Yet we do it. Until we die to this, we are not truly free. It takes dying daily to everything we want and are, to accomplish this, then becoming alive to Him.

Intimate presence with our Holy Bridegroom Lamb is necessary for this. Knowing Him intimately is our inheritance. We do not have to say a prescribed prayer, stand on one foot, and hold our mouth a certain way. We must continue to move toward Him. When we seek Him with all our heart (broken and messed up though it is) we will find Him. (Jere. 29:12) He made us for this intimacy. We were created for this freedom from controlling our destiny. Above everything, as a bride, He created us for complete surrender.

With what lies does a sexual abuse survivor live? Many blame themselves and ask, "why me". They live in monumental shame and debilitating pain. The shame and pain are based on lies. It is ludicrous to believe being abused is your fault, yet we do it.

How about someone constantly told they were stupid, ugly, worthless, talented, or better than anyone? We can become narcissistic or self-denigrating because of our experiences. Both can control our destiny as the driving force of our lives.

Perhaps your choice to avoid conflict with angry people is to retreat into passivity. You may tell yourself and others you don't care or "I will not bother with this". You look at the" You look at the angry person as the sinful one, the problem. Passivity and anger are both caused by fear. Both are sinful.

How about a victim of violent crime? In what way, can a victim stop seeing himself or herself as a victim? Is it possible for slavery and pain to benefit us?

The process of slavery should make us disgusted and angry enough to question the reality by which we guide our lives. When we cannot go on in our present condition, we are finally ready to hear the truth.

My Story Again

After the wounding years' shame and pain blazed like a roaring fire but somewhere within me was a small ember. What was it? I did not know.

But I had questions. Why? "Why did I suffer at this level," was the unanswered question. Now I see the self-seduction and self-deception and the desire to control Him and my destiny are what He was pursuing. In fact, we humans try to control our destinies.

My heart cried out during this time, "But Lord, I obeyed you. Why did obedience result in this destruction within me?" I was obedient, but I also needed to be dead to everything that kept me from true intimacy. I needed to know what motives allowed me to be ensnared and deceived by the many false words that move through the church. He allowed me die to my thoughts of how everything worked in life because what I believed filtered through my "stuff".

Yet healing of the debilitating pain did not come till close to 8 years after He showed me the desire to control my destiny. Restoration and the rest of the healing took 21 years. Why did He wait so long? I still do not know. One thing I understand is only He heals us.

Only after He took the pain did I realize that shame caused the pain. They heaped the shame upon my life during my growing-up years and even more during the wounding years. Further, I was so used to living in shame I did not know it was the pain until He removed it.

The other thing I realized was to survive and function, I had to bury the pain that came from the spiritual abuse my family endured. I lived for years with buried pain. I also buried the passion, but had not known it. That was the ember that I could not identify. Until He healed the shame, knowledge of the ember eluded me. Now passion needed resurrected, so I could feel what God feels. However, passion for Him cost me everything.

One day, in talking with my husband, I told him I realized I buried the passion. He said he had as well. Neither one of us knew how to let it live again. We cried as we talked as we realized we had buried passion. We threw ourselves on God and asked Him to restore. This was challenging because it was the passion that caused the persecution. (Song 8:1) This was risky but His will brings His presence. We were counting on this.

Pharasaical Self-Deception

The next incident shows the attitude of the Pharisees and its effect in keeping them from seeing who Jesus was. Self-deception filled them.

John 9:1 "As he went along, he saw a man blind from birth. 2 His disciples asked him, "Rabbi, who sinned, this man or his parents, that he was born blind?"

John 9:3 'Neither this man nor his parents sinned, "'said Jesus, "but this happened so that the work of God might be displayed in his life.

John 9:4 As long as it is day, we must do the work of him who sent me. Night is coming, when no one can work.

John 9:5 While I am in the world, I am the light of the world."

John 9:6 Having said this, he spit on the ground, made some mud with the saliva, and put it on the man's eyes.

John 9:7 "Go," he told him, "wash in the Pool of Siloam" (this word means Sent). So the man went and washed, and came home seeing. "

John 9 is an example of the Pharisees believing lies and living as if they were true. They did not recognize Jesus because of their beliefs about the scriptures. Their teaching said if a man was born blind, either he or his parents were terrible sinners. They also knew what Messiah will look like when He came. The motive was fear of displeasing God and being taken captive again as they were when they became captives in Babylon. They became captives because of sin. The Pharisees felt that if they had enough rules, the rules would keep them from displeasing God. Instead, their extra rules separated them from God because they were based on fear and fear causes idolatry. Because the idols were not wood or metal figurines, they did not recognize them as idols and neither do we.

The Veiled Woman

Song 1:7-8 "Tell me, you whom I love, where you graze your flock, and where you rest you sheep at midday. Why should I be like a veiled woman beside the flocks of your friends? If you do not know, most beautiful of women, follow the tracks of the sheep, and graze your young goats by the tents of the shepherds."

In this process of seeing the slavery we cry out as Shulamite did. *"Where do you graze your flock, and where do they rest during the heat of the day?"* There is recognition. Somewhere is a flock tended by the Lord that is different somewhat from experience. Shulamite has been as a veiled woman. The lies put a veil between her and her lover. She wants an end to the veil, an end to working at midday in the worst heat, an end to being involved with a flock that will only use her. The Bridegroom tells her to follow the tracks of the sheep. The scripture says, *"My sheep hear my voice."* She needs to find the sheep that are hearing His voice, not the lies of the enemy. Although few, there are sheep that hear His voice. If she seeks, she will find them. Even if she doesn't come across a whole church or a collection of them, a few close friends will be enough.

Now she must listen to His voice. It is His voice she must hear among the sheep. This is difficult. As former slaves come together with the Shepherd, the old lies still have power. Sometimes former slaves will find themselves back under slavery again. Freedom increases as the truth increases. Former slaves must hear God. Then freedom will grow. Further, they must know Him in the secret place. True unity is born there. We first experience unity with Him, then with His church. The answer to bigotry, hatred, and injustice, both financial and social, cannot be solely addressed through programs, although they can be beneficial. We find answers to these things in the presence of perfect unity, our Triune God. As our hearts unite with His and we hurt for what He hurts for, we will find ourselves united with those who are one with Him. Out of unity that is birthed in His presence we will find the calling He has for us to bring His unity to our world.

John 17:20 "My prayer is not for them alone. I pray also for those who will believe in me through their message, 21 that all of them may be one, Father, just as you are in me and I am in you. May they also be in us so that the world may believe that you have sent me. 22 I have given them the glory that you gave me, that they may be one as we are one: 23 I in them and you in me. May they be brought to complete unity to let the world know that you sent me and have loved them even as you have loved me."

The glory He gives us is the glory of His presence and Bridal love, as we are in the Secret Place with Him.

So how do we receive the new word from our new Father that was mentioned earlier? II Corinthians 10:4-5 gives us the answer.

Our Weapons

"The weapons we fight with are not the weapons of the world. On the contrary, they have divine power to demolish strongholds. We demolish arguments and every pretension that sets itself up against the knowledge of God, and we take captive every thought to make it obedient to Christ."

Some worldly weapons are lies, guns, and retaliation. These are not our weapons. Our purpose is not to destroy people but to demolish pretensions and arguments (lies). These lies set themselves up against an accurate knowledge of God. If the lies reign, we have a distorted view of God. In fact, we will see Him through the lies. We overcome lies with truth. We cannot cast out a lie. Nobody has the power to silence it. It won't cooperate. We must replace it with the truth.

When faced with a lie that is a reality for us, we must search the word to find a scripture that contradicts the lie. A concordance helps in this search. Another way is to ask the Lord what scripture we must stand in. When we find a scripture that lives, that is quickened to the heart, we have our weapon.

Is the lie now dead? No, but we have a weapon to use. The soul needs time to accept the new word. Every time you notice that the lie is speaking within, speak the new word. You might have to say it a dozen times until it becomes real to you again. In time, the new word takes the lie captive. Your thoughts will become obedient to Christ. (See Chapter 9 for more on freedom from the lies.)

What is a Doer?

James 1:21-25 calls it being a doer of the word. *"humbly accept the word planted in you which can save you. Do not merely listen to the word and so deceive yourselves. Do what it says. Anyone who listens to the word, but does not do what it says, is like a man who looks at his face in a mirror and after looking at himself, goes away and immediately forgets what he looks like. But the man who looks intently into the perfect law that gives freedom, and continues to do this, not forgetting what he has heard, but doing it - he will be blessed in what he does. "*

The word planted refers to a seed rooting itself in the heart. If we plant the truth in the heart, it will choke out the weeds of the enemy, the lies by which we live life. Listening to the words, or mouthing the words, "God is love." leaves us with deception in the heart about God. Perhaps you believe God is out to get you. One day, during many trials, you realize you feel this way. You run to the scripture and look up a verse about His love. Saying it aloud helps you feel better for a few hours or days. But soon you arrive at the same place. You wallow in it. In fact, you decide the scripture is no help and quit. You are the man who looks at His reflection and forgets how he looks.

Is there a way for someone to forget what they look like? It becomes simpler if you choose to believe misconceptions about yourself and God. You forget the truth you saw concerning the problem within because the lie is more real.

The text mentions a man who looks intently at the perfect law. This man studies the scriptures. When He sees something in his life that is a lie, he looks up the scriptures that relate to his problem and stands in them. A few hours later, when familiar doubts come back, he stands in that scripture again. To look intently means to see the details. Despite not feeling the truth in his soul, this man chooses to believe God by examining the scripture. This is not a name it, claim it theology. It is purposing to believe. Then the truth destroys the power of the lie.

Notice the perfect law gives freedom; the lie brings bondage. The man looks intently and "continues to do this," remembering what he heard. In fact, what we all need to forget are the lies. What we need to remember is the truth.

This person who does what the word says is as the King James' Version calls him, a doer, or a poet. That is what the word doer means. A poet inspects words, works with them, and extracts every ounce of meaning from them. A doer does the same. When the doer comes to the word, in God's presence, knowing the mind of the Lord is the purpose. Further, the doer waits on the voice of the Lord by His Spirit to open the meanings of scripture. This process takes days, weeks, months, and years. Believing the lies took years.

A renewed mind gives us two things. First, we will know God. We will know Him as Bridegroom. We will perceive His essential being. Second, we will know ourselves. The lies will no longer define Him, nor will they define us to ourselves. We will, as the scripture says, know the truth that sets us free.

Does this sound like work? Slavery is more work.

Seeing the lie is painful. It is difficult to part with it because it is a part of who we are, our identity. It is familiar. This is the only reality we know. If we give it up, what will we have then?

The truth.

We will simply have the truth.

Now we understand God. We thought we understood Him before, but He was a god who looks like us, or dad, or Uncle Joe, and Grandma, or a slightly improved version of the best person we know. He resembles the people we hold in awe. He also resembles what the preacher said in his sermon. We saw Him in types and shadows when we heard the word and observed life through our lies. Now we hear of Him through the sheep that hear His voice, and we hear of Him from Himself by His voice and through His word. We learn to enter His chambers, His secret place. We give up our types and shadows and perceive Him in truth. That's right truth.

The Secret Place

Lamp stand, shew bread, only types of Him
into whose presence, I must now come.

Not trusting in the ritual of the stand and bread,
but looking unto Him in that secret place.

Putting aside all types and shadows,
facsimiles, and caricatures of Him.

What my mind thinks will not suffice.
My eye must behold Him in the secret place.

Then I will know who He really is.
Not just what men would say
or types and shadows show.

And I will learn to be content in Him,
only in Him.

What is the importance of this new word from our new Father? This was answered above in part, but there is something further to consider.

The Wedding

Psalm 45:8-9 (The beginning of this passage describes the Bridegroom.) *All your robes are fragrant with myrrh, and aloes and cassia; From palaces adorned with ivory the music of the strings makes you glad. Daughters of kings are among your honored women; at your right hand is the royal bride in gold of Ophir."*

In the prophetic sense this wedding is THE wedding. The bride is there with Him. His robes have spices upon them that are in the anointing oil and incense. Each of these spices speaks of His death. Later, we will look at the full significance of this when we study the wedding in Song of Songs. It is enough to note that His wedding and His death are inseparable.

The bride is at His side and she is told this:" Listen, O daughter, consider and give ear: Forget your people and your father's house. The king is enthralled by your beauty. Honor him for he is your Lord."

The bride is hearing a new word. She is to forget the past. Forget the lies. Forget the old word from her old father. She is to leave behind what her father's house represents. Above all, as we continue our study, you note that the spiritual consummation cannot take place until the bride forgets her father's house. We cannot go on into true intimacy with the Lord if we hold to the past lies.

There are many places we can stop along the way in the Song of Songs. While we might comprehend Him as Savior by staying in them, we won't experience the depth of knowing Him as a husband.

When he saves us, we are betrothed engaged. In Hebrew society, the engagement was as binding as the marriage. Until the wedding ceremony there is no deep intimacy. If we stop along the way unwilling for the intimacy, then we will miss the most glorious purpose of our salvation. We were not only saved from sin, and He is not fire insurance. Rather, He saved us for himself, to know Him and fellowship with Him at the deepest level possible, bridal intimacy.

In our society intimacy, has become synonymous with sex but they are not synonymous. Intimacy means to understand one's deepest nature. He has called us to perceive His essential being, to understand His deepest nature, and to allow Him to know us in the same way. Yes, He knows us that way now, but He wants us voluntarily to make ourselves known to Him. This requires an end to hiding behind the lies. Intimacy is only possible in an atmosphere of love, vulnerability, and truth. Those who protect their lies do not have intimate relationships. They are not vulnerable, truthful or love well. The lies hold others and our Bridegroom at arm's length.

Those who press in deeply are not an elite group. They are not better than others. They have known Him better and they walk in a closeness of relationship, not because He plays favorites, but because we do. We play favorites when we choose the lies over Him who is the truth. We play favorites when we remember our father's house.

The past was ugly, yet He sees her beauty. She enthralls him. It is a beauty free of her past life. Forgetting her father's house is to honor Him. To forget her father's house is to be ready to enter His house, His chambers.

To forget
is imperative
to marry Him.

Renewed
The mind,
a court jester
standing on his head
crying inside

living a lie.

Humility's mask falls off
revealing the face of pride.
Self is crowned
upon the throne.

But then
His words descend upon the lie
the tears dry
mask discarded
a renewed mind.

For Reflection

1. Do you value life lived in His presence more than anything life can offer? Do you ache to have time alone with Him?
2. Ask the Lord to show you a strategy in warfare and write down what He says. Then fight for your own freedom and the freedom of others as you are ready.
3. Write what God is saying to you about the new word from your new Father.
4. What weapons of the word of God and prayer can you use to fight for freedom.

Prayer

Mighty and Holy God, I stand in awe of your power and glory. Forgive me for playing games with this life you have given me. I have not understood the wonders of your presence. I often treated you as if you were only slightly powerful and as if you winked at sin. My heart has not desired you above all else. Draw me Lord, into your heart. Help me seek you alone. Help me want you more. Don't abandon me to my own ways. Reveal the idols in my life. Rationalization and self-deception keep me from seeing them. Expose everything that keeps me from knowing you. Help me quit trying to control my destiny and trying to control you.

I want to see your sacrifice correctly. Prepare me as your bride. I want to know your heart. Reveal yourself to me and transform my life. Move in me so I will make you my "Everything".

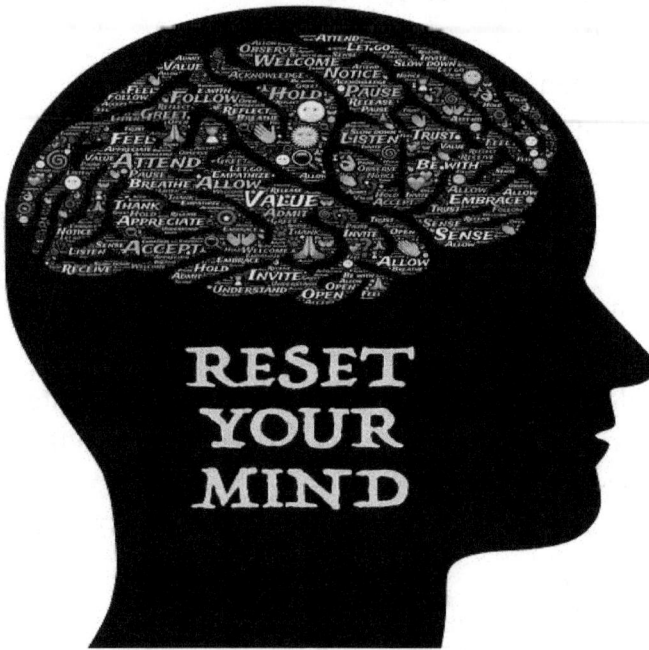

RESET YOUR MIND

Chapter 8

His Table

His Chariot Horse

Has our bride become free of her past? No. In the last chapter, she recognized the need to hear the voice of her Beloved. She committed to putting her past behind her and knows that only in His presence, hearing and loving Him, will she be able to say goodbye to its power. In fact, she decided for Him, but the outworking of that decision takes time.

The bride grapples with His Lordship. Again and again, she will need to commit to His Lordship. Giving up her agenda is part of the cost she will pay for intimacy with him. To help her on her way, the voice of her lover speaks.

Song 1:9 "I liken you, my darling, to a mare harnessed to one of the chariots of Pharaoh."

What a strange thing to say. Recently set free from slavery, He tells her she is a horse. She is not any horse, though; she is a mare. A mare is a female horse that is mature and is breeding age. She has come through a terrible time and needs encouragement. He wants her to know He sees her as one who has the potential to be fruitful and mature. Indeed, the bride is a candidate for marriage.

She is a chariot horse for Pharaoh. A chariot is a symbol of power. Pharaoh had the best chariots and the best chariot horses of the day. They had stamina in battle, strength, and beauty. She has become a warrior. He sees the stamina she has developed during her time of slavery. This is the first time in Song of Songs we see her as a warrior, but not the last. She learned about fighting the lies of the past as well. That is the beginning of real warfare. She must engage in this warfare daily because the lies of the past are persistent. To be seen as a warrior at this point is wondrous to her. She hardly knows what she is doing, but the Lord sees her potential.

2Cor. 10:3 "For though we live in the world, we do not wage war as the world does.

2Cor. 10:4 The weapons we fight with are not the weapons of the world. On the contrary, they have divine power to demolish strongholds."

2Cor. 10:5 "We demolish arguments and every pretension that sets itself up against the knowledge of God, and we take captive every thought to make it obedient to Christ."

Warfare for the bride is not done with a gun or a sword. The weapons the Lord provides have divine power. This divine power is far beyond what most of us understand. It demolishes strongholds. Strongholds are ways of thought that the enemy has set up in our minds. These strongholds rule our thought life. We do not realize that some ways of thinking are a problem until the Lord convicts us.

Through the Lord's divine power, we can demolish these strongholds and every pretension (lie) that exalts itself against our knowing God. Every stronghold is based on lies. One of the major weapons we must use against the stronghold is the truth of the word of God. We must retrain our mind to no longer accept the enemy's lies. This means we must take our thoughts captive to make them obedient to Christ through the word of God. This causes reading, study and memorization of the word. Concentration must be regularly on scriptures that speak against the wrong ways we think. Concerning this, see the next scripture.

Goal: the Enemy Finds Nothing in Me

John 14:30 "I will not speak much more with you, for the ruler of the world is coming, and he has nothing in Me;" (NASB)

As an illustration think of a property owned by one person. The property is called Redeemed Territory. In the middle of that property is another plot of ground called Enemy Territory owned by another person. For the owner of Enemy Territory to access his land, he will get a legal right of way. The right of way gives the Enemy Territory owner the right to cross the Redeemed Territory land to access his middle property.

When we come to Christ, we have a great deal of territory in our soul that still takes direction from the enemy. The goal is to take away all legal rights to enemy territory and the right of way to cross Redeemed Territory. To accomplish this, we must quit agreeing with the owner of Enemy Territory.

When Jesus died, the enemy came, but he had no hold on Him, no property rights, unlike us. The goal of each believer's life should be to give no property rights to the enemy. No enemy territory.

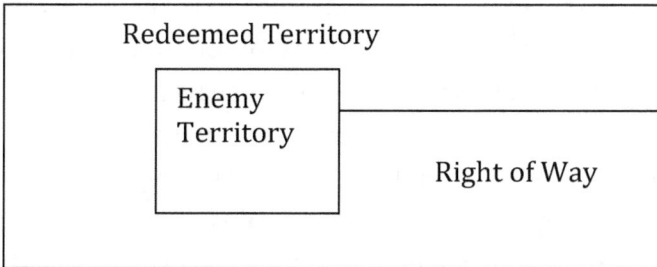

Along with giving no place to the devil, we must also put on the Armor of God.

Eph. 6:10 "Finally, be strong in the Lord and in his mighty power.

Eph. 6:11 Put on the full armor of God so that you can take your stand against the devil's schemes.

Eph. 6:12 For our struggle is not against flesh and blood, but against the rulers, against the authorities, against the powers of this dark world and against the spiritual forces of evil in the heavenly realms.

Eph. 6:13 Therefore put on the full armor of God, so that when the day of evil comes, you may be able to stand your ground, and after you have done everything, to stand.

Eph. 6:14 Stand firm then, with the belt of truth buckled around your waist, with the breastplate of righteousness in place,

Eph. 6:15 and with your feet fitted with the readiness that comes from the gospel of peace.

Eph. 6:16 In addition to all this, take up the shield of faith, with which you can extinguish all the flaming arrows of the evil one.

Eph. 6:17 Take the helmet of salvation and the sword of the Spirit, which is the word of God.

Eph. 6:18 And pray in the Spirit on all occasions with all kinds of prayers and requests. With this in mind, be alert and always keep on praying for all the saints. "

We are told to "be strong in the Lord and His mighty power". His mighty power is beyond our understanding, yet we are told to be strong in it. The next instruction is about how we do this. We are to put on the full armor of God to overcome the hierarchy of demonic rulers in the heavenly realm. The words used in verse 12 give us the rank of various demonic forces. The words show rulers and lesser powers. They are organized like an army against humans and against the Lord's church. We must not be ignorant of this fact. The next verse says *"Therefore"*, because of this ranking of the spiritual forces of evil in the heavenly realms *"put on the full armor of God, so that when the day of evil comes, you may be able to stand your ground, and after you have done everything, to stand. Stand firm." Eph. 6:14.*

We not only must resist the enemy, but we must stand firm and when we have done all to stand firm, we are still to continue to stand firm. Sometimes the battle is so fierce we only hold the territory we have won back. The point at these times is to not give up the ground we fought to win. And if you have given ground back refuse to let it stay in enemy hands. Or perhaps you slipped into an old behavior and feel shamed by your failure. Don't listen to the lie of the enemy. Stand your ground in the word of God. The enemy's false narrative insists there is no hope or freedom for you, but it's a lie. God's word is true.

Types of Armor

Then Eph. 6 lists types of armor. Some are defensive, and some are offensive. We are to stand firm with the belt of truth around our waists. Truth holds all else together. Truth is essential for the rest of the armor to function. Without this belt, the robe worn by soldiers hinders them. The robe of the warrior tucks up under the belt, allowing the warrior to fight more freely. Without the truth transforming our lives we will keep on stumbling over our "stuff". Without the truth, we would believe the enemy's propaganda and never get free.

The breastplate covers the heart. We should let the breastplate of righteousness, purchased by Jesus, safeguard our hearts and defend us against present attacks that hinder our progress. We must come to recognize that because of His blood, we are His righteousness. This is not through our merit, but His. Because of this, we are to accept His help when temptation or verbal attack comes to our lives. We need to walk in His righteousness rather than the sin that so easily besets us. When we put on the breastplate, the revelation of His imputed righteousness aids us in our warfare.

Then we are instructed to put on the shoes of peace. We must have shoes run on any surface and not injure our feet. These shoes are the shoes of peace because the gospel brings peace between the sinner and the Lord. We are to walk in the peace the gospel brings to the heart because the peace He came to give extends to any who will receive it.

Next, He tells us to use the shield of faith and extinguish the flaming arrows of the enemy. In the day this was written, the enemy shot arrows, and they stuck in the shield as the warrior raised it in defence. The enemy shoots flaming arrows at us daily, tempting us to fall back on behaviors destructive to our new life. This is true when someone hurts us or comes against our loved-ones or us. We are to raise the shield of faith against these arrows. This shield has the power to extinguish all flaming arrows and stop them from killing our spiritual life. To have faith, we must renew our mind with the word of God.

Next, we must take the helmet of salvation. This is another defensive weapon. The helmet protects us from the thoughts that the enemy desires to use against us. We need to understand all that Christ purchased for us through the cross. As we study and pray to understand these great truths, the Lord will help us. He will renew our minds through study and prayer until our thoughts come in line with His thoughts.

Offensive weapons

The next weapon is an offensive weapon, the sword of the Spirit, the word of God. We wield the word of God in hand-to-hand combat as a sword. Often, we judge our situations by our circumstances. The kingdom coming in our situations is not dependent on our circumstances. Instead, we demonstrate the kingdom through our faith and the power of God's word, rather than being swayed by our circumstances. The word kills the enemy's plan and purposes.

This sword is double-edged and is a dagger per (Strong's 3162). We used a dagger face-to- face combat. The battle is this close.

The word of God functions at two levels. One is Logos. This means "something said (including the meaning)." [v] Scripture is one example of this. The Lord Jesus in John 1 as the Word of God is the Logos of God. The Word spoke and created the world.

God speaks the word to us as "rhema" (Gk). This is a quickened word or "an utterance". [vi] The Spirit of God speaks this to us at the moment we are taking part in a prophetic hearing of the voice of God. This type of hearing is available to all believers. He desires to speak to us face to face. Amid warfare, we need both Logos and Rhema. The scripture instructs us and helps us resist the lies of the enemy. The speaking voice of our Lord helps us know how to apply the scripture to our present circumstances. In the secret place as we meditate on the Logos, often the Rhema is spoken to our hearts. Both sides of the sword cut away the lies and set us free.

Another offensive weapon is praying in the Spirit with all kinds of prayer. By perceiving the spiritual realm during the use of the word of God and prayer, we would witness the forces of darkness shrinking back in fear of the offensive weapons given us by the Lord. Sometimes it takes prevailing prayer to overcome our enemy. That is why we are told to pray with all kinds of prayer and petition. We must not limit the Lord, but be led by Him in our praying. If we are not led by Him and stop short: we will not see the victory He died to purchase us. Being led by Him means we listen to Him for His strategy in warfare. We spend time in the secret place with Him and move forward as He directs. By keeping our focus on Him and His guidance instead of our circumstances, we are empowered to move forward in faith. He knows the strategy of the enemy and wants to show us how to counteract it. Complete defeat of the enemy may be a lengthy process, as He seldom discloses more than the next step. We need intimate connection to our King, so we do not stop short of victory.

The next instruction is to be alert and keep on praying. We are not to fall asleep, but to stay alert. We are not to disengage from the battle, but keep on praying for all the saints. There are no vacations from spiritual warfare unless the Lord grants them.

The enemy attacks at inconvenient times and we need to be alert. We will not struggle with being alert if we stay connected to the Lord. We will be ready for anything that comes.

Warfare Through Worship

Warfare also takes place through worship.

> Psa. 149:1-9 *"Praise the LORD.*
>
> *Sing to the LORD a new song, his praise in the assembly of the saints.*
>
> *Let Israel rejoice in their Maker;*
>
> *let the people of Zion be glad in their King.*
>
> *Let them praise his name with dancing*
>
> *and make music to him with tambourine and harp.*
>
> *For the LORD takes delight in his people; he crowns the humble with salvation.*
>
> *Let the saints rejoice in this honor*
>
> *and sing for joy on their beds.*
>
> *May the praise of God be in their mouths*
>
> *and a double-edged sword in their hands,*
>
> *to inflict vengeance on the nations*
>
> *and punishment on the peoples,*
>
> *to bind their kings with fetters,*
>
> *their nobles with shackles of iron,*
>
> *to carry out the sentence written against them. This is the glory of all his saints. Praise the LORD."*

The first verse of this passage above speaks of singing a new song unto the Lord. It's a song for worship that is provided ahead of time to be incorporated into worship. It might also be a spontaneous song introduced during the worship service. This author was in a service where someone sang a song they had never sung before. There were verses and a chorus. A singer sang the verse and when the singer started on the chorus, the entire assembly sang the chorus. This was a song they had never sung before. The same person who sang the first verse sang the second verse and the entire assembly sang the chorus again and so on. This was a new song no one ever heard before, led by the Lord Himself, who knows how to help us war.

Verses 6-9 above speak of praises of God in their mouth and a two-edged sword in their hand. The two-edged sword is the word of the Lord. The word that God is currently speaking cuts both ways. His word is the power that created the world. This will bind nobles and kings. It stops the demonic powers actions. Prophetic worship overcomes barriers that keep the Kingdom of Heaven from being manifest on earth. The bride is a prophetic warrior.

Another type of prayer is petition. He tells us in I Th. 5:16-18 to pray continuously. Since prayer changes things in the heavenly realm, this causes quite a few victories if we practice this type of prayer. Continuously suggests a connection ongoing throughout the day. This can be difficult amid busyness, but if we will commit to turn our thoughts to Him, it is possible. We can also set aside specific times to give our attention to petitions.

Eph. 6:18 encourages us to *"pray in the Spirit on all occasions with all kinds of prayers and requests."* This is very like 1Thess. 5:16-18.

Submission and Resistance

Phil. 4:6 Do not be anxious about anything, but in everything, by prayer and petition, with thanksgiving, present your requests to God. This passage speaks of prayer and petition and adds *"with thanksgiving"* the entry way to praise and worship.

We find another principle of warfare in *James 4:7 "Submit yourselves, then, to God. Resist the devil, and he will flee from you."* You notice we must first submit to God, then resist the devil. Success in warfare is impossible without obedience. If we resist the devil without submitting to God, we will not have the power to overcome the enemy's plans.

Our Lord is not an elected president. He is the King of Kings, the absolute ruler. Obey means to "prescribe by statute, to submit to[vii] "So first we submit to the King. This means we give up our will and ideas of how life works. We do this knowing that His will is best. Then we resist the enemy.

The meaning of resist is "to stand up together, to resist (or assault) jointly rise up together (with God). [viii] We are not alone in this battle. We are called to rise as God rises. He is Emmanuel, God with us. He assures ultimate victory. Thus, we have no excuse for not joining in the battle for the desires of His heart. We need to understand we are NEVER alone in warfare. If we say, "I resist you Satan," we are standing with God in it. If we think we do warfare in our faith, they can overcome us. We do warfare in His finished work.

Sometimes we war better when we are new, passionate and naïve. As we walk out our life in Him, we see our shortcomings and we doubt our ability to overcome. However, we must push through the doubt and unbelief. To do this, we must seek the Lord until we know we have His heart in the matter before us. With His heart comes the faith that goes beyond our abilities.

He also sees the bride's potential to be fruitful when He calls her a mare. Though she cannot see it yet, as she engages in warfare to possess her own soul, she will give birth to spiritual children and mentor them. Because of the destruction in her life, this is an amazing statement. Next, He describes her hearing.

Hearing His Voice and Christlikeness

Song 1:10-11 Your cheeks are beautiful with earrings, your neck with strings of jewels. We will make you earrings of gold studded with silver."

Earrings speak of hearing the voice of God. He has noticed that she now hears His voice. The gold is His perfection and silver His redemption. He has graced her with both that she will hear Him and know His heart.

Some ways to hear His voice include reading His word, the Holy Spirit's witness, circumstances, internal promptings, sermons or conversations, books, and both difficult and blessed experiences.

He speaks of her neck being adorned with jewels. Jewels speak of the attributes of Christ. In place of the slave yoke, she has His beauty adorning her. Translators elsewhere rendered the word earrings in verse 11 circle. That suggests He makes a crown for her. It will be gold (His divine nature) studded with silver (His redemption). She not only has His beauty where the slave yoke once was, but now upon her head, the place where the lies prospered, she will wear His perfection and redemption. She will find in time God redeems her thoughts and perfects them. The lies within her will shrink away because she will learn to resist the devil and he will flee from her.

She has only recognized the initial steps she must take to leave slavery behind her. Her mind is still often in a whirl of confusion because of her past, though she has committed to freedom from it. He sees her with his beauty. The decision she has made, not the battle she is still fighting, defines her identity. He sees her through the eyes of eternity and tells her who she is in Him.

His voice is her stability.

His truth is her freedom.

His word is her dawning reality.

Song 1:12 "While the king was at his table, my perfume spread its fragrance."

What does the king's table, perfume, slavery or freedom from slavery mean? A great deal. The king's table that Shulamite reclined at was lavish, with many servants scurrying about her. Remember what happened with Solomon is a small part of the picture.

In contrast, this is the Lord's song. His table is different. Many are seated; there is a large banquet. His table is full of blessings, provision even as Solomon's table, with one difference. This is the Lord's Table. The main course is the broken bread and poured out wine. He was the true food, but more than that, He served the meal to the disciples and washed their feet. This is the table to which the bride comes.

King and Servant of All

John 13: 1-5, 12-17 'It was just before the Passover feast. Jesus knew that the time had come for him to leave this world and go to the Father. Having loved his own who were in the world, he now showed them the full extent of his love. The evening meal was being served, and the devil had already prompted Judas Iscariot, son of Simon, to betray Jesus. Jesus knew that the Father had put all things under his power, and that he had come from God and was returning to God; so he got up from the meal, took off his outer clothing, and wrapped a towel around his waist. After that, he poured water into a basin and washed his disciples' feet, drying them with the towel that was wrapped around him.

When he had finished washing their feet, he put on his clothes and returned to his place. "Do you understand what I have done for you?" He asked them. "You call me 'Teacher' and 'Lord,' and rightly so, for that is what I am. Now that I, your Lord and teacher, have washed your feet, you also should wash one another's feet. I have set you an example that you should do for one another as I have done for you. I tell you the truth, no servant is greater than his master, nor is a messenger greater than the one who sent him. Now that you know these things, you will be blessed if you do them."'

Washing of feet was necessary in that day for sandaled feet became dirty. This was the job of the lowliest slave. However, the Lord of Glory, our Bridegroom, washed the feet of the disciples. Then He served them their first communion, taking the place of both slave and sacrifice. He even washed the feet of Judas our Lord's betrayer.

The bride sees these truths at His table. She sees that only through becoming His will she be free from slavery. It takes her death to receive the life of God. Being last brings promotion.

Meanwhile, over in the corner, the disciples are arguing. *Luke 22:27 "Also a dispute arose among them as to which of them was considered to be the greatest."*

Wait, a minute. Does this suggest the disciples had this argument while He was serving them? That is unbelievable. Two verses after He washed their feet and served the cup, they were arguing about who was the greatest. Ridiculous, right? This is worse than ridiculous. That is slave talk. If you desire greatness, men's opinions carry too much weight. Others can enslave someone who worships men's opinions. The Lord's Table is a confusing place. We see Him serve while the rest of us jockey for position.

Hear what else He has to say, *Luke 22:25-27 "The kings of the Gentiles lord it over them; and those who exercise authority over them call themselves Benefactors. But you are not to be like that. Instead, the greatest among you should be like the youngest, and the one who rules like the one who serves. For who is greater, the one who is at the table, or the one who serves? Is it not the one who is at the table? But I am among you as the one who serves."*

Slavery has two participants, the slaveholders or benefactors, and the slave. Slaveholders put themselves in the position of benefactors. The attitude the disciples exhibit in this passage could bring them into slavery or into the authoritarian attitude of a benefactor.

The disciples still have much to learn. However, in a matter of weeks, they were transformed. How did it happen? Jesus died. He served them to the end. Then they understood.

It is in returning to His table again and again that we finally get the message. Losing is winning, death not an end, a beginning. Brokenness is the only way to wholeness. Letting go of slavery to men and idols brings us to commit to serve Him completely as He served us. We become His slave. The Greek work for slave is doulos. [ix] In some translations, doulos is rendered servant.

The following passages include the word doulos rendered as servant but with the literal meaning of slave.

Gal. 1:*10 "For do I now persuade men, or God? or do I seek to please men? For if I yet pleased men, I should not be the servant of Christ."*

Phil. 2:7 "But made himself of no reputation, and took upon him the form of a servant, and was made in the likeness of men:"

Rev. 15:3 "And they sing the song of Moses, the servant of God, and the song of the Lamb,"

A slave has no rights, and they are subservient to their master. Jesus took this position to show us how He served us by dying for us. Also, to show how He served us by making intercession for us. He calls us to be subservient to His will, and, in contrast, find the greatest freedom and joy imaginable. He calls us to be His doula, His slave.

The Bride's Fragrance

At this place, the bride's perfume spreads its fragrance. This is the same perfume we read about in verse three of Chapter 1. That which anointed Him for burial is now upon the bride. The alabaster box containing the perfume must be broken for this to occur. Moreover, the bride must be broken and poured out to give off the fragrance of His perfumes. His table is imperative to this breaking. He will bring her back as often as He must till, she is so broken she will never try to manipulate another life or win the favor of mere men. Then He will bring wholeness to her she never thought was possible.

Song 1:13 "My lover is to me a sachet of myrrh resting between my breasts." The myrrh sounds personal. It is. This must happen in a hidden place. The breasts of the bride signify ministry and nurturing. Myrrh signifies death. The Bridegroom's death between the breasts of ministry alone can cease her desire to be a spiritual superstar and put an end to ministering, with impure motives. Only the death of our Lord can compel the passive person to leave their hiding place and fulfill their purpose in the kingdom. No more wanting everyone to say how wonderful she is in her service to others. No more hiding from potential. Instead, she experiences death to the hidden motives of applause, recognition, and manipulation of lives. There is death to fear that causes hiding. His death in her brings death to performance and the fears that motivate service, either self-aggrandizement or fear of serving.

The myrrh is in a hidden part. Only she and the Bridegroom know it is there. She does not wear it publicly so that others exclaim over how dead to self she is. Have you ever heard an acquaintance, yourself, or a speaker tell how dead to self they are? That is myrrh worn for others to see. She does not use knowledge of scripture to make it appear as if she is dead. She is the only one who knows it. Then she quietly dies.

Hosea 2:2 "Let her remove the adulterous look from her face and the unfaithfulness from between her breasts." If myrrh does not rest in the ministry, harlotry will. The effects of harlotry are devastating. Many ruined lives float in the wake of a ministry that draws attention to self.

King Saul had an outward anointing without the inward brokenness. Without the inward work, he was an envious, harsh king who hunted down broken men like David. He was not dead to self, but lived for self. The center of his universe was Saul. Kingship was an open door to fame, not service to God's people. Power was his desire, not brokenness. (I Samuel 8:5-31:13)

The presence of people like Saul in the church has been constant. God is calling a people who have languished under the crushing heel of Saul like slaveholder leaders. More broken men and women will comprise the next generation of leaders. There have been many arrogant slaveholders to do the breaking.

We need these arrogant leaders. They are our testing and proving grounds for genuine humility. The bride will meet up with people like this throughout the whole of her earthly journey. She is learning how to respond by letting His death do its work in her soul and in her ministry, so she will not beat

God's sheep, too. However, without the brokenness of the persecution she has endured, she would become another Saul. God prevented this through struggle.

The temptation after coming through a time of difficulty is to build walls. In fact, most people have walls to keep others out to protect oneself. This is true when betrayal is a part of the pain. The thought is one must stay distant to keep from being hurt. Jesus did not handle betrayal this way.

When He chose Judas, Jesus knew Judas would betray him. Nevertheless, He continues to disciple Judas and shows the same love and regard He shows the other disciples. Jesus did not build a wall. Walls are not a righteous way to deal with hurt.

Walls and Shields

A part of my story may help here. After being betrayed more times than I want to count I was destroyed. I wanted to avoid more hurt for a season because I needed to heal. So, I found I could not share my past with people. Talking about the past invited more wounding. I stuffed the pain down and shared with others only the things safe to share.

As I headed toward healing, I had a burning question. How do I build walls against the type of people that had hurt me? I had no natural walls. Being tender hearted and a transparent person made me vulnerable. They used my willingness for correction and my honesty many times to wound me. I needed to do life differently.

One day, as I shared this with a friend, she hugged me and prayed. As she did, the Lord reminded me that Jesus did not build a wall against Judas. He did not protect himself from His betrayer but served him.

Now a new question arose. "If not a wall, Lord, then what?" That night I had a dream in which a shield played an all-important part. The next morning, I woke up with a song about the Lord being my shield I had not sung in 20 years. Later that day, I was sharing with my boss about a man who worked for me. He was a dangerous man and used intimidation whenever he talked with leaders. I told my boss I did not know what to do when that happened. My boss said that if someone verbally attacked him, he would imagine a big Plexiglas shield surrounding him. Then the words bounced off the shield. I got it. The Lord is my shield if I will let Him be.

> Psa. 3:3 But you are a shield around me, O LORD;
>> you bestow glory on me and lift up my head.
>
> 2Sam. 22:3 my God is my rock, in whom I take refuge,
>> my shield and the horn of my salvation.
>
>> He is my stronghold, my refuge and my savior—from violent men you save me.

Ugly accusations that come our way are the blazing arrows of the enemy. The Lord is our shield if we trust him. Arrows stick in or bounce off the shield of faith and trust. Trust in Him requires that we die to our walls and sinful ways of relating and throw our entire future and everything we desire on Him.

This description of His table we have just looked at is only a glimpse of His sacrifice. Therefore, the bride does not see clearly what He did for her. It only feels like a distant concept until she endures her own share of His suffering. She must experience the depth of His death in her.

Dove's Eyes

Song 1:15 "How beautiful you are, my darling! Oh, how beautiful! Your eyes are doves."

Now the bridegroom speaks of the beauty He sees in her. This beauty has to do with her having doves' eyes. A dove is faithful to one mate for life. She is not looking for another lover or diversion. Her eyes are fixed on her beloved. What does it matter what men think, if she pleases Him? She looks for one thing, the smile of His face. A dove also has no peripheral vision. She keeps her eyes straight ahead on her beloved instead of circumstances or the praise of men. This is something she learns more in depth over time.

Song 1:16 "How handsome you are my lover! Oh, how charming! And our bed is verdant."

Verdant means green with growing plants. *Psa. 23 "He makes me lie down in green pastures."* The bride has a place of rest. It is just a place along the way, but so necessary to being able to complete her journey to wholeness.

Her life is still intense. Sitting at His table smashes so many of her theological boxes. Much that she trusted in is gone and it takes time to replace it with truth. She struggles daily with the tendency to think like a slave. No clear definitions of who she is or who God is remain for her. Everything important in her life is being redefined. She is learning a new way of thinking and being.

Her travail and confusion are expressed here:

Bits and Pieces

Bits and pieces of life
come floating through my mind.
One of God
and one not,
O Lord
help me find,
the way to you
the way for which
you purchased me.

Which bit, which piece?
Father heal my blindness
that I might see.

Cause me to know
your upward way
moving ever toward

your throne.
That my redemption
now complete
I would be your
very own.

Your face I long for,
your glory I would see,
that I might understand
 all that you are,
and all that you
 ever will be.

 Your sovereignty I will not trifle with
but bow unto your will.
I stop struggling in your hand
and remain very still.

Bring forth Oh God
your life and light
dispel the darkness and death.
I bow before your way Oh Lord,
my God
 who gives me breath.

 Come forth in me,
come forth in me
my heart now breaking cries!
 Now you forever my portion be
lift me to the skies,
to the place of rest,
the place of peace,
the place of your mighty throne.

 It happened,

at long last it's done
And now I am forever your own.

Song 1:17 "The beams of our house are cedars; our rafters are firs."

Cedar is a type of His sinless humanity. No worm invades cedar. The beams upon which the house is built, the foundation for their relationship, is His sinless humanity. No bride exists if He was not human and sinless. There would be nothing but slavery forever. Even the cedar of their house speaks of His sacrifice.

The fir tree is an evergreen. His sinless humanity is the foundation for everything in His kingdom, and His eternalness holds the roof up. He does not have to die again. He already died once for everyone. She has confidence in His promises. They will come to pass. He has done what He will do. She does not need a sign. A miracle will not save her, but abiding in the eternal sinless one will. She found hope in his death as a slave.

Poured Out
He came with nail-scarred hand
to serve the royal band.
He walked on nail-scarred feet
to take the lowly seat.
 And then poured out His life
to take us for a wife.

For Reflection
1. In what areas are you aware that you struggle in relationships?

2. How important is it to hear His voice? What results from not hearing His voice?

3.What holds you back from knowing Him intimately?

4. What does it mean to make Him Lord? How does knowing him intimately help you make Him Lord?

5. What lessons of warfare do we learn from the following scriptures:

2Cor. 10:3-5-taking thoughts captive

Eph. 6-Armor of God

Psa. 149-warfare through worship

Eph. 6:18-petition

Phil. 4:6-anxiety and petition

James 4:7-resist and submit.

6. How do you resist the devil? How do you submit to God?

7. Listen to the Lord about who He sees when He looks at you. Write in your journal what He says.

9. How much of your identity do you receive from what others think of you?

10. How much of your identity do you receive from what the word of God says about you?

12. Look up scriptures in a concordance that will help you understand who He says you are. Write them in your journal. Listen over the next weeks for God to bring other scriptures to your attention and write them down and memorize those that speak to your need.

Prayer

Lord, I so need you. I worry about so many things. I make people's approval more important than it ought to be. Vigilance in warfare needs to become a bigger priority. The propaganda of the enemy guides my life too much. I want to hear your voice and to know you.

I do not understand the vastness of your love for me. Life teaches you are small, like men. You are not like men. We are made in your image, but sin has distorted that image. Help me see you. Help me know you. Only you have the power to disclose your true self to me. I want you to be Lord of my life. Teach me what that means.

Help me learn to war according to your will. Show me how to resist the enemy and submit to you. Show me the areas where my will is in the way and help me yield to you in each of these areas. Draw me, Lord, into your presence so you can revolutionize my life.

Help me see the lessons you have for me in Saul experiences. Heal the pain from these experiences. My focus sometimes dwells on what happened. Move me beyond this until all I can see is you with me, training, loving and teaching me.

Chapter 9

The Betrothal Banquet

The Rose of Sharon

Does the bride have wholeness? No. All we looked at in the last chapter she is learning, but not mastered. They are the realities; however, she lives in partial reality. She knows the scriptures well enough to understand that they are truth, but part of her soul does not believe it yet. Her experiences still shaped her point of reference. Song of Songs shows the type of experiences the bride must experience to come to wholeness. She needs a new word from her new father, and she also needs a new history as well, a history with the bridegroom in it.

Song 2:1 "I am a rose of Sharon, a lily of the valleys."

The rose of Sharon is the Narcissus, pretty, but small, insignificant and not lasting long. The lily of the valley grows among the standing grain. This flower has multicolored blooms and strong stems used as fuel for heating. This is a common flower.

The bride is still in crisis. She has seen the Lord in an additional dimension. Her heart is turning away from those behaviors that have caused her to be a slave. Her many years of slavery and hurt inflicted by the slaveholders were great. Healing takes time.

Suffering has shown her wrong reactions to her persecutors. She, too, sometimes wants to be the greatest. He finds her beautiful, but she sees the fleeting beauty of the ordinary Narcissus, here today, gone tomorrow. Similarly, though possessing lovely flowers, she is only fuel for the furnace like the lily.

Moreover, God's blessing seems far distant. Years of persecution cause her to expect only difficulty. The Lord has shown her the purpose of the difficulty, but her heart has not caught the message. She accepts rebuke as her due, but receiving the Lord's love is something that seldom happens. The other voices tell her she does not deserve it. Someday those voices will be still. The more she responds to Him reaching out to her, the less power those other voices will have.

His reply: *Song 2:2 "Like a lily among thorns is my darling among the maidens."* She is a lily for the burning as He was. Though a lily, she is as a flower among thorns. Compared to the other maidens, she is far superior. Her insignificance is like the Lord's that caused people to overlook who He was. People don't notice persecuted servants. They notice people important in their own eyes. However, He notices her.

The bride has good soil in her heart, but thorns flourish in shallow soil. Thorns exist to cause pain to those who encounter them. They also make glorious crowns for crucifying kings. The bride is planted in the valleys of difficulty where the good soil is abundant.

Song 2:3 "Like an apple tree among the trees of the forest is my lover among the young men." Now the bride compares the Bridegroom to others. He is a fruit tree among the other trees that have seed, but no edible fruit. He is the fruitfulness of the tree of Calvary.

Did you realize that at any point in your Christian life, you have a choice of trees? Since the Garden of Eden, we had a choice of trees. We could eat of any tree except the tree of knowledge. Knowledge of what you may ask. Good and evil, right and wrong. We decide based upon our knowledge, what is good or evil, right or wrong. This knowledge leads to pride, since we believe we know something. It leads to judging; after all, we are right. It leads to gossip, and strife and every evil among us.

In contrast, the Garden of Eden was about fellowship and intimacy with God. We chose the tree of knowledge and lost intimacy with Him. So, He sent the heavenly Bridegroom to die on a tree. He did not die of natural causes. His death was not an accident. No one stoned Him. He died on a tree and gave us a choice of the tree to which we would look. Other trees look good, but they have no food, no fruit. They are trees of knowledge that lead us in mental circles and always bring us back to worshipping ourselves. We then think more highly of ourselves than we ought to think because other trees are devoid of the knowledge of God.

Additionally, when we partake of the fruit of Calvary, Jesus Christ, we partake of God. He becomes one with us, and we become one with Him. We lay aside the knowledge of good and evil and embrace knowledge of Him. This process is not one and done. Would that it was. The knowledge of good and evil has made great inroads into our minds. We must continuously choose the one fruit tree. This is a lifetime work.

Part of her past is this tree of knowledge. As she learns to choose the one fruit tree, her past becomes dimmer and dimmer. It is this struggle with her past that strengthens her and causes her to seek Him with desperation.

When Adam and Eve chose the tree of knowledge in rebellion against the Lord's explicit command, two things entered the human experience. These guide and bind our lives today. The first was shame. Prior to eating the fruit, the man and woman were naked and not ashamed (Genesis 2 and 3). After eating the fruit Adam hid himself because he was afraid. He feared because he was naked. So first he suffered shame because he was naked, then he became afraid. Indeed, the first fallen human emotion was shame and, the second was fear. Shame and fear are the entrance point for the enemy's work in our lives ever since the Garden. We will look more at fear and shame in the next chapter.

Double Minded

At this point the bride has experienced the death of the Lord. Everything she has seen in Him speaks of death. She knows what scripture says about resurrection, but it is not real in her own heart because the time of resurrection has not yet come to her. When the Lord resurrects her, then she will find more fullness of victory. Over the years, the effects of shame and fear will become less and less. Moreover, resurrection will manifest through her.

Have you ever seen someone in this stage? They are double minded. They want God but are still fearful. The struggle with fear is one of the principal occupations of their life, but their success rate is not constant. Since they often have bouts of depression, we may try to fix them. We tell them about the scriptures they already understand, to convince their hearts of the realities they must embrace. When they discover a truth, we may say in disgust, "Well, I told you that two years ago. You never listen to me."

The truth is they may have been listening but are unable to hear. Past voices take time to be stilled. In this case, double-mindedness is the war between the old and new.

Have you ever heard someone say, "You should be over that by now?" That is a common frustration among those who watch this wounded, confused bride struggle. There is a saying today; "It isn't over till it's over." Only God knows when this struggle ends. The reason we want the struggle over is, so our lives can be more convenient. It is no fun to be around someone in this struggle.

We must pray for them, and they must pray constantly and cry out to God to come to wholeness. Our past hurts: our brokenness, and our crying need for healing are the way we become a praying people. It rarely happens without this process.

If we accept the difficulty and pain of change, we will learn to pray. If we will not accept the difficulty and pain of change, we will never become a praying people. We will become instead, a people who try to circumvent pain and never come to wholeness.

Love and Obedience

Song 2:3b "I delight to sit in his shade and his fruit is sweet to my taste."

The bride has learned to sit in the shade of His tree and partake of the fruit. The fruit of that tree is so vast that books and books are written about its benefits. She may be a semi-frightened, double-minded bride, but she knows where to feast. Laying aside the other tree and the strife and pride it engendered, she chose the fruit of His tree. His fruit is humility, peacemaking, meekness, and a host of other things. She made a choice despite her confusion. That choice ensures the wedding day comes.

Does she know what is coming when she makes the choice? She hopes feasting on His fruit will qualify her, but she does not know in the center of her being yet. For her there is no other choice. Returning to total slavery is unthinkable. Going forward is to live in terrible pain for an unspecified length of time. The question forms, "What if the pain never stops?" The voice of the past tells her the pain is incurable. Not willing to go back, she is afraid to go forward. As she partakes of His tree, she is reminded of His suffering and makes the right choice out of love and obedience.

Sometimes all we have is love and obedience.

Sometimes that is enough.

The Betrothal

Song 2:4 "He has taken me to the banquet hall and his banner over me is love."

Picture this: the cottage sets back from the road surrounded by grapevines. Wind blows up dust in a small yard. A strikingly beautiful young woman steps into the doorway, her flowing robes swinging. With flashing eyes and the flutter of browned hands she said, "He is coming, Mother, he is coming."

"Then come in here and be dignified. You must not appear so eager."

"But Mother, it is exciting. There is a lovely procession with him and he's wearing his royal robes."

"Then welcome him in the door, dear."

"Come in," Shulamite said, motioning with her arm toward the interior of the simple room. Her parents trembled slightly at the table.

The king stepped inside. Suddenly, the familiar room seemed too small. He wore a purple robe with a jeweled crown on his raven black hair. His features were strong, with a chiseled chin and a determined set to his mouth. Walking toward the table, he set a scroll, a box, and a bottle of wine. Then he sat with a flourish, spreading his robe behind him.

"I have come with the marriage covenant," he said, extending the scroll toward her parents and turning to smile at Shulamite. His face softened, and love shone in his eyes as he drank in the sight of her. He did not look at the humble room. His eyes never left her face.

"Everything appears to be in order," said her father as he finished reading the scroll.

As Solomon turned his head slowly to look at her father, he said, "And here is her price, " as he slid the ornate box across the table and opened the lid.

The eyes of her parents opened wide as her father stammered, "But my king, her price is not that high. How can I accept this?"

"If you study the marriage covenant, you see that her price is my life. The contents of the box are only a token."

He turned to Shulamite as he poured wine into her glass. Handing her the glass and looking into her eyes as they drank deeply of the wine, he said, *"This is my covenant with you."*

In the illustration, the banquet hall in verse four literally means banquet of wine, the betrothal banquet. A Jewish man would bring the price of the bride, a copy of the marriage covenant, and the wine. The King of Kings has betrothed Himself to us in love. The price of that love was His life. He signed the contract in His blood.

Matthew 26:26-28 'While they were eating, Jesus took bread, gave thanks and broke it, and gave it to his disciples, saying, "Take and eat; this is my body. Then he took the cup, gave thanks and offered it to them, saying, "Drink from it, all of you. This is the blood of the covenant, which is poured out for many for the forgiveness of sins.'

The wine used at the banquet of wine is a symbol of His blood. His body and blood were the price of the bride. He has taken her to the betrothal banquet and His banner over her is love.

In fact, the new covenant in His blood is the marriage covenant. It is not some other covenant. He bought us with a price to marry us, not just save us from sin. We need to emphasize this truth within the Church. Without it many stay spiritual babies. Often, we emphasize pet teachings and ideologies. We must keep the Lord central. We must preach Jesus Christ crucified. Our preaching should include the Lamb in the midst of the throne and the Bridegroom, who awaits us.

When the scripture talks about the Church as a bride, we are never called the bride of Christ. Though it is intimated in Ephesians 5, bride of Christ is not specifically given as a name. Scripture calls us the wife of the Lamb. *Revelation 21:9b "Come, I will show you the bride, the wife of the Lamb."* If we are ever to fulfill our highest calling, it will be as the wife of the Lamb that was slain. If we are to know Him in truth, then we must know Him most through His suffering and death, His cross and ours. That makes us a faithful wife. That prepares us to rule and reign with Christ.

When a Jewish man was betrothed, he returned to his father's house to prepare a place for his bride. Often this meant adding on rooms to his father's house. *John 14:1-3 "I go to prepare a place for you. And if I go and prepare a place for you, I will come again, and receive you unto myself; that where I am there, you may be also."* When Jesus said this to his disciples, he was talking as the Bridegroom to the bride. Moreover, he paid the price for us and then went to His Father to prepare the bridal chamber. He said this just before He died.

Song 4:b "His banner over me is love." The banner is a flag. The flag of this King is love. He carried this standard into battle and won the victory of the cross because of love. It is His love alone that can encourage His people to war and be victorious over the enemy. If we hang back from the conflict, we do not understand His love. We need a fresh vision of His sacrifice. We must have a fresh infusion of His love and grace so that we might mount up with His flag flying before us. His sacrifice enables us to fight the enemy until His works in our lives and the lives of our loved ones are finished.

This means we must have a continual revelation of His sacrifice throughout our lives because the enemy never stops. We see that death most clearly as we face suffering. A life without difficulty is lived in ignorance of His great sacrifice and indescribable love.

Song 2:6 *"His left arm is under my head and his right arm embraces me."* This is a picture of the last supper with the disciples, the betrothal banquet prior to the coming forth of the bride, His Church. John reclined against the Lord on that Passover celebration. He was the disciple who yearned for intimacy. That is the heart of the bride when she sees His sacrifice. All those who desire the closeness that John knew are, "the disciple whom Jesus loved."

His sacrifice alone ignites our love.

His death was our bridal price.

Not just the price of our salvation.

It was the price of love.

For Reflection

1. Is He the ONE fruit tree to you, or do you embrace the idols that result from seeking knowledge?
2. Will you commit to allow Him to re-educate you according to His will?
3. When you enter to battle, is it out of frustration with circumstances or love for others and God?
4. Ask Him for a new revelation of His bridal price. Write what He shows you.

Prayer

Lord, I need you more than I know. I am too self-absorbed and self-sufficient. I think I have life figured out. Too often I do not realize how far off I am from your truth. Take me back to your table and teach me the truth. Help me connect with the one fruit tree, the tree of love, and quit serving shame and fear. Forgive me for trying to gain your approval through the things I do. Help me to only do as you are leading me. Help me understand you are the point of this life, not the fulfillment of my dreams. I am helpless to change without you. Have mercy on me and lead me.

**FREEDOM
IS OUR
BIRTHRIGHT**

Bride's
Heart

Becoming The Bride Of Christ

5 STEPS TO A TRANSFORMED MIND

GAL. 5:1 FOR FREEDOM CHRIST HAS SET US FREE

Click the link or type in your browser to get your free book. Or just join me on my website.

https://www.bridesheart.com/

Chapter 10

The Bride's Tomb

Our Tomb and His Hiddenness

Song 2:8 The voice of my beloved! Behold, he comes,
leaping over the mountains, bounding over the hills.
Song 2:9 "My beloved is like a gazelle or a young stag.

She hears His voice and knows He is coming. Jesus told us that His sheep know His voice. In His day shepherds put their sheep in a pen with many other herds. Since sheep look alike, this could be a problem, but when the shepherd calls out, his sheep separate themselves from the others and follow him. Scripture tells us they will not follow another. This is a covenant statement.

God allowed the Israelites to be taken as captives to Assyria. *2 Ki:18:12 Because they obeyed not the voice of the LORD their God, but transgressed his covenant," KJV.*

We think of the Old Covenant as a list of do's and don'ts, but it was much more. God expected obedience to His voice. His voice was the issue as Jeremiah shows us in chapter 7.

Jer. 7:22 For I spake not unto your fathers, nor commanded them in the day that I brought them out of the land of Egypt,

*concerning burnt offerings or sacrifices: 23 But this thing
commanded I them, saying, Obey my voice, and I will be your God,
and ye shall be my people: and walk ye in all the ways that I have
commanded you, that it may be well unto you. KJV.*

The story of Israel's refusal to hear the Lord's voice for
themselves is in Exodus 19 and 20. God offered them His voice,
but they wanted Moses to speak on God's behalf, so He gave
them the law rather than His voice speaking to each person.
Instead of pursuing a close relationship with God, they chose a
system of law that proved difficult to follow. Walking with God
has and is about obedience to His voice. Despite selecting
human intermediaries and the Law, God continued to
communicate with those who will listen. We see David, Samuel,
Josiah, Asaph, Joshua, Caleb, the prophets and many unnamed
others. Those who listen are His sheep and the bride listens.

When He comes, He has infinite power and grace as He
leaps over the mountains of difficulty and the hills of suffering.
She, on the other hand, still gets laid low by difficulty. But the
bride notices how He handled Calvary and knows she must
become like Him. Then she describes His abilities further. He is
graceful like a gazelle or a young stag. The word gazelle means
beautiful or splendor. So, she sees His glory as He is on the way
to her. Then she sees something else.

*Song 2:9 My beloved [is] like to a roe, Or to a young one of
the harts.*

Harts have uniquely split hooves that enable them to scale
vertical rock surfaces by finding minor defects to grip onto. No
mountain is too difficult for the hart. He climbed the mount of
Calvary but before that He scaled the Pharisees, the Mount of
Olives, Gentile leaders and torture. He was surefooted, and we
are to become like Him. Paul talked of being like Him in His
death. Phil. 3:10.

Next, she speaks of a wall between them.

*Song 2:9b Behold, there he stands behind our wall,
gazing through the windows, looking through the lattice."*

Her wall is constructed of her false beliefs about Him and life, her painful past, family generational problems, difficult relationships, and things important but not good for her. She desires closeness but cannot have it because the wall she calls our wall has its origins in her. She sees Him looking at her through the windows on the other side of the wall and gazing through the lattice which keeps her from seeing Him clearly. The veils she hides behind are like a lattice obscuring him. This is true in her growth here, but see what scripture says is her legacy. One day, the veils will be gone.

2Cor. 3:18" But we all, with unveiled face, beholding as in a mirror the glory of the Lord, are being transformed into the same image from glory to glory, just as from the Lord, the Spirit."

The glory of the gazelle she sees on Him will one day transform her as she beholds Him. For this to take place, the wall must be removed, but how does that happen when He continues to be not quite reachable? Though the text does not show the passing of time, we know that the transformation of a life takes decades or at least many years. The wall of her past shuts her off from Him except for glimpses for a long season. This puts her in the tomb. Others call it a tunnel with no light at the end and others a long, dark time.

The Bride's Tomb

In the following section, we will discuss the tomb, and everything related to it. *Song 2:10 "My lover spoke and said to me, 'Arise my darling, my beautiful one and come with me'."*

Arise means she has been out of commission for a season. While she could be asleep, she is actually crushed and waiting for resurrection.

Song 2:10, is the Bridegroom's call to the bride to come forth from the tomb. His call is for her to move beyond past pain and sacrifice her own desires, so that she may one day fully embrace His will and find true life. Before we investigate the bride's tomb, which is also your tomb, I want to tell you about my tomb and His death.

I was in the tomb a long time before I understood where I was. The death was obvious. Dying is an event filled with activity. The tomb is known for its lack of activity. Dead people occupy tombs. Dead people do nothing but lie there.

My ministry was dead.

My expectations of God's people, dead.

My ideologies, goals, aspirations, and desires, dead.

Only my heart was alive, and it was broken.

Broken by relentless spiritual abuse,

broken by my wrong ways of understanding suffering,

broken by the Bridegroom, who loved me,

broken by my sin.

Tombs are airless, solitary, dark, unwanted, and part of God's plan. Even if there was a large crowd around me, I felt alone. No one could reach me. Not the real me. That person became entombed, yet I had to keep working and taking care of the people in my life. What others saw was the façade I wore to continue breathing in and out. God crushed my identity. If I opened my mouth, the pain rushed out. How could I explain what I no longer understood?

Alone and awaiting resurrection, yet not knowing resurrection was coming, I believed I would lie alone forever, no longer known or sought for. Resurrection is something that happens to others. No one else has the ability to reach me except for the Lord, who can bring resurrection.

Man could do nothing for me.

Man caused the tomb.

Or did he?

The tomb engulfed me, making me feel as if I had been swallowed by the depths of the earth. Gone were the things I once trusted in. I felt as if the tomb had destroyed the beliefs I held dear. He was mine, but He was not noticeably present. I gave everything for my love for Him. Love was asleep, numb, like a severe wound with no pain when the body is in shock. It was time to wait, to survive, to breathe. For what was I waiting? I did not know, but the next move was His.

Ironically, I wrote the main body of this book while in the tomb in 1992. That is 19 years from the time I am writing this paragraph. At the time, I wrote this manuscript; I thought I the tomb ended since God was so present as I wrote. The manuscript flowed from my heart. I wrote about the resurrection because I thought I was living through it. I was not. The resurrection did not begin until 2001. This was the first phase, healing the shame and pain from the wounding years and my childhood. I waited 10 years for the first phase and 20 years altogether for my life's resurrection.

The attacks that occurred over the years had hurt me deeply. I did not understand how I became so damaged. Where was the way to life without this awful pain? I did not know I suffered from deep shame. I couldn't connect with books that depicted shame. For 10 years, I cried out for the pain to be healed and I asked God to show me what shame was, so I might understand it. One day, while reading *The Wounded Heart* by Dan B. Allender defined shame in a way that made sense. I couldn't perceive how it manifested in my life, but I came to understand the shame I must have felt because of the profound pain. Understandings of the tomb years are below and woven throughout this book. Yes, some of our deepest learning comes while in the tomb. The death we die when we suffer in His sufferings bring life one day.

Love and Fear
x The Garden of Eden contained the tree of life (brings love) and the tree of the knowledge of good and evil (brings fear). He

calls us to be "perfected in love", (I Jn. 4:18) but thoughts from the fear tree hamper us.

1John 4:18*"There is no fear in love. But perfect love drives out fear, because fear has to do with punishment. The one who fears is not made perfect in love. "*

God's perfect love when received casts out all fear. The problem is we have eaten so much fruit from the tree of knowledge we do not relate well to the perfect love of God. Therefore, we continue in fear, and fear brings torment (punishment) to our minds. We are in a prison of thoughts that keep us vassals of the many gods we have constructed through the tree of knowledge and the many years of serving various fear gods. Our desire to control our lives comes out of the fears we serve.

For a plant to come back year after year we may need to keep the seed and plant them or it i a self-sowing plant. In the fall, just before winter, the self-sowing plant produces seeds that fall to the ground. The next spring, when pleasant weather comes, the plant grows. This growth takes the death of the seed, which turns into a sprout. The sprout grows and looks completely different from the seed. Yet, the materials for the plant, existed within the seed, though invisible to anyone who looks.

So, we can understand fear and shame as the season of fall and winter and death. Giving and receiving love and knowing others value us are the seasons of spring and summer. Whatever type of thoughts we plant will spring up within us. The seeds of fear and shame also produce a crop, though they are from the winter seasons.

Love and Fear

Fall and Winter Death /Fear	Spring and Summer Life/Love
Fear of Exposure/shame LU 2:2-12	"For me to live is Christ," Phil. 1:21
Fear of abuse Rom. 8:15, 2 Ti.1:7	Perfected in Love Jn. 4:18
Fear of Man Prov. 29:25	Fear of the Lord - Prov.14: 27
Fear of Rejection- LU 13:49-53	Bride has made herself ready -Rev.19:7
Shame-Is. 47:3, Is. 54:4 ,Jere. 20:18	I am valued-Song. 4:7

Shame results from one's dignity and worth being attacked. We turn people into objects, so we can use them and speak about them without guilt. We then believe they deserve what they get.

Some objects are:
- Object of verbal abuse-idiot, stupid #*@!&* are objects.
- Sexual abuse-pornography and dating ideas turn people into objects.
- Religious abuse- the term rebel can justify religious abuse.
- Envy of another ministry or person turns another believer into a rival. A rival is another object.
- Bullying-Is tormenting another object to make oneself feel bigger or better.

- Rape-This is impossible unless the person an object of lust, control or fantasy.

- Exposure for poor behavior–This results in being treated as an object of gossip.

- Object of rejection- the person experiencing this is turned into an object, judged as deficient. They are not enough or believe they are not enough.

What is the worst shame women could experience? Look at the definitions of shame below in the original Hebrew.

Shame Definitions

These definitions are from Strong's Exhaustive Concordance and include the Strong's Numbers.

"2781 *kher-paw'*; from 2778; contumely, disgrace, the pudenda:—rebuke, reproach(-fully), shame.

6172.*er-vaw'*; from 6168; nudity, literally (especially the pudenda) or figuratively (disgrace, blemish):—nakedness, shame, unclean(-ness).

2834.*khaw-saf'*; a primitive root; to strip off, i.e., generally to make naked (in disgrace) make bare, take, uncover."[xi]

The word shame means to strip bare or make naked in disgrace. Inherent in each of these definitions is the female genitalia reflected in the word pudenda. This word is in the female form, not the male form of the noun. So, shame means to strip bare as in a woman being stripped bare. Every woman knows if she is stripped bare, rape most often is the result. In most cases, she can do nothing to stop it. Shame, in this context, is especially fearful. But shame happens to men as well. It is also devastating. Men can feel stripped bare and humiliated. When shame reaches this intensity, it damages male or female.

Fear is such a small word, only four letters for such a colossal problem, such a big god. Shame initiates fear. Fear of being exposed as deficient. Fear results from being naked and *"being clothed in shame" Job 8:22*. Like Adam we search around for fig leaves and find shame and the fear of exposure that clings to them. "Everyone knows the deficiency," is screamed into our soul. "You are outcast, an object of ridicule, judged as no longer human." FEAR consumes joy, kills hope, and crushes destiny.

Job 10:15 If I am guilty—woe to me!

> ***Even if I am innocent, I cannot lift***
> ***my head,***
> ***for I am full of shame***
> ***and drowned in my affliction.***

(Emphasis mine.)

Shame fills us and colors everything. It is the lens through which we view the world. We struggle in relationships because we are looking through a fear lens at the people in our lives. It is hard to trust if you are afraid of being exposed and shamed. The affliction of shame is so pervasive it can bring death to our effectiveness even when the shame was undeserved. Fear of future shame and the attendant pain that comes with it keeps us from embracing the cross as it comes to our lives. We believe we suffered enough. Where is the break from suffering, we cry? Because we do not understand a correct response to shaming actions toward us, we become more wounded than we need be.

Psa. 44:15 My disgrace is before me all day long,

> *and my face is covered with shame*

We struggle with this disgrace because the pain is so huge. Shame covers our minds; disgrace is in the forefront of our lives even if we shove it down, so we can function. As a result, we have trouble lifting our heads to look others in the eye.

*Psa. 4:2 How long, O men, will you **turn my glory into shame**? (Emphasis mine)*

*How long will you **love delusions and seek false gods**? (Emphasis mine)*

This problem often starts in our families of origin and becomes the filter through which we judged everything. Shame comes when a child feels alone and abandoned. This sets up a lie of unworthiness to receive love. That is a shame, thought.

This does not mean we must abandon the child to feel this. Shame-based parents have behaviors that can, without thought cause that sense of abandonment. Each of us can only do the best with our children based on the light we have today. We do this no matter how much we desire to protect them from our own hurts.

Shame encourages us to seek solutions to our problems that cause us to cling to idolatry. We fear more shame. We fear exposure again, so we do everything in our power to keep that from happening. The false god of self-defense receives our service. Elaborate constructions keep people at bay, so no one can hurt us this way again. As we do this, we are not allowing God to be our comfort or our protection.

We believe our behaviors protect us. Life trained us to despise our desire to be known and loved by either a certain class of people or everyone we encounter. The belief that our desire is our enemy, and we must do our best to kill it, to wall in our heart, cuts us off from the possibility of love. Our actions shut out God and the people He sends into our lives that would help heal the past pain. We are self-deceived and self-deluded and seeking these false gods we have constructed.

The Lord asks us how long we will turn His glory into shame. Our fear of man shames God, so does our idol worship. God is shamed by our addiction to shame-based thoughts. We become like that which we behold reverently, by that which we rehearse. Shame keeps us from His image because it and the fear attendant with it fill our vision. We worshipfully behold our fear and cling to it as if it can save us from future hurt. Yet all it promises us is that we will never receive the Love of God or others while fear and shame rule in our lives. And we cannot love others with these idols active in our lives.

Psa. 97:7 All who worship images are put to shame,
those who boast in idols—
worship him, all you gods!

The sad fact of our plight is that we are so wounded we believe we must protect ourselves. We do not trust God. Idolatry demands that shame be a continuing cycle. Idolatrous worshippers that do not allow Him to protect them are put to shame. They do not see that one day when every knee bows the gods of this world, the gods of self-defense, fear of man and fear of rejection will worship Him. The shame-based person rarely knows they are serving these false gods. They view life through shame. This person has no consciousness of this orientation, coloring everything.

Fear causes idol worship. Fear, awe and worship are the same word biblically. What we fear we give awe to that belongs only to God.

So, what is the answer? If you have a stronghold of fear and or shame, cry out, stand in the word of God for your deliverance. Memorize scriptures that tell you the truth about God, relationships, shame and fear and especially who you are in Christ. Put the weapons of prayer and the word of God to work for your sanity and your intimate relationship with God and his people.

Trust

Psa. 25:2 "in you I trust, O my God. Do not let me be put to shame, nor let my enemies triumph over me."

Speak this scripture or another like it to your soul until it is more real than your experience. Refuse to continue to live at the corner of Fear and Shame Streets in the town of Idolatry.

Psa. 34:5   "Those who look to him are radiant;
*   their faces are never covered with shame."*

Notice that those who look to the Lord, who trust in the Lord, are radiant rather than covered with shame. *"their faces are **never** covered with shame."* (Emphasis mine.)

In Matt. 9: 20-22, a woman touches Jesus, and she is ashamed. She was desperate because of bleeding for 12 years.

This made her unclean, an outcast. According to the law, if she touched anyone, they will become unclean. Cleaning her house was to render it unclean. She refrained from attending community events or socializing with friends for fear of contaminating them. The Pharisees of her day taught that her problem and others like it were caused by sin. This woman knew shame. Seeking relief, she reached out to Jesus and trusted in his ability to heal, and he did.

For 12 years, the woman suffered. The number 12 is the number of authority. This woman was an outcast, and, in a moment, Christ's authority set her free. She went from unclean sinner to healing and authority in a moment. Now she could tell her testimony to anyone without it causing them to become unclean.

Psa. 71:1In you, O LORD, I have taken refuge;
let me never be put to shame.

He alone is our refuge. No one else can defend us from the evil deeds committed by men except for him. We cannot protect ourselves, for that only leads to idolatry and grieving His heart by our lack of trust in Him. When we trust Him, if someone puts us to shame, it will not stick to us and change us into idolaters, for our focus is on Him. If we behold shame and fear regularly, we will worship them. If we behold Him with reverence amid fear and shame coming against us, we will become like Him. The next verse says it well:

Psa. 71:3"Be my rock of refuge, to which I can always go; give the command to save me, for you are my rock and my fortress. from the grasp of evil and cruel men."

Why do we need to fight? What do we gain besides our sanity and the ability to be true worshippers of the only one deserving worship? We have a grand future and need to embrace the promise of it to help us as we give up our idolatry.

We need to become militant as we fight for our wholeness because the following is part of it.

Rev. 19:6 "Then I heard what sounded like a great multitude, like the roar of rushing waters and like loud peals of thunder, shouting: "Hallelujah!
For our Lord God Almighty reigns.

Rev. 19:7 Let us rejoice and be glad, and give him glory, For the wedding of the Lamb has come, and his bride has made herself ready. "

We give Him glory when we worship Him alone. *"The bride has made herself ready."* The bride has set aside idolatry and the protections the world and the enemy of our souls offers. As a bride, she has become completely vulnerable to her Bridegroom. Vulnerability is necessary for consummation. Despite any shame that comes her way, she can triumph because she knows she belongs to Him.

Rev. 19:8 "Fine linen, bright and clean, was given her to wear.(Fine linen stands for the righteous acts of the saints.)"

The bride receives her wedding garment from the Bridegroom. She embraces His way of doing things. As a result, she lives righteously, becoming more and more like Him. He becomes her refuge instead of hiding in unrighteous self-protection. The bride opens to love and to the possibilities that love provides. She makes conscious choices every day to turn her eyes on Him and not on past or present circumstances.

Rev. 19:9 "Then the angel said to me, "Write: 'Blessed are those who are invited to the wedding supper of the Lamb!'" And he added, "These are the true words of God."'

Those He invites He blesses. Blessed are those who take part in the Lamb's wedding supper. This supper is the prime point of history. There will be no shame. There will be no idol worship. He is the ultimate culmination of everything.

The Gift of Suffering

Phil. 1:29 *"For it has **been granted** to you on behalf of Christ not only to believe on him, but also to suffer for him,"*

The word granted as used in Phil 1:29 means gift or charis (in Greek). This is the same word for the gifts of His grace mentioned in Corinthians 12. Suffering is a gift of His grace as much as a word of knowledge. Another gift is when a preacher is preaching, and you know God just spoke to you. Suffering is a gift, just as it was when He died. By His death, He interceded for us. This was spiritual warfare of the highest level. Sometimes our suffering is warfare on behalf of His kingdom. We love to talk about the gifts of healing or prophetic preaching, but we do not recognize what a gift suffering is to us. Suffering is how we become like Him. It is the way we give up the behaviors that keep us from knowing Him intimately. Suffering tears down the wall that separates us from Him.

Now we begin the narrative of the bride's tomb.

Song 2:7 "Daughters of Jerusalem, I charge you, by the gazelles and does of the field: Do not arouse or awaken love until it so desires."

This is an accurate picture of the bride's heart. Love for Him cannot be aroused or awakened until it desires. Desires what? Desires Him. The bride never loses desire for Him, but the price of desiring Him in the past was all, everything. It is time for the heart to lie numb and broken for a season. She will yearn for Him again. The tomb must do its work. The longer time she spends in the tomb, the more glorious the resurrection and the greater the love she will have for Him as the tomb imprints the lessons of dying, in the deepest recesses of the heart. Time for reflection is plentiful. Some deep learning takes place here, though the bride will feel she is learning nothing. In reality, she is learning how to stay dead, how to survive the loss of everything. She is learning the importance of her will becoming His will.

What then did she lose? It must have been something precious to produce this profound effect. No, it was not valuable, at least, not to God. He is the one that made sure she lost it. To her, though, it was life. Her identity, however false it might be, is gone. What takes its place?

Trust in Ideals

Her problem has been one of trust. In whom or what has she trusted? If you asked her, she would have said she trusted the Lord. That is the correct theological answer, but not true. Each believer trusts in their own ideals, expectations, and opinions much more than they trust in God. They trust in them until they die. Dead people don't have ideals, expectations, and opinions.

The dictionary tells us that an ideal "exists as a mental image, or in fancy or imagination only:" [xii] In other words, we might call it an idol of the mind. Notice it exists in the imagination only. That means we bring with us ideas of how life ought to be that exist only in our minds. This is where the false identity lives as an idea that exists only in our minds. These ideas have no basis in reality. This is true for our personal lives and our corporate life as a church. We often guide our lives more by ideals than we do by truth. And we expect others to live up to our ideals for the Christian life. We then measure everything based on the ideals we cherish and protect. The church, when doing this, adds things that are tests of the genuineness of faith. These tests are based on external actions. This presents a performance-based criterion, that then ensnares the saints and keeps them from authentic relationship with the Lord.

The religious life is prone to this. We can read one scripture and form a new ideal because we interpret scripture based on our ideals. Ideals cause us to put expectations upon others and upon God. We expect both man and God to act as we have idealized. Since our basic premises are wrong, idealism must die for us to see God as He is and see our brothers as they are.

Real Versus Ideal

Another word to consider in this context is the word real. Real refers to that which is permanent. It is not an illusion. It is not fraudulent. Rather than clinging to ideals, we are to become real. We are to lay aside our illusory idols.

In the New Testament, the word truth means, "not concealed"[xiii], in other words, real. Contrast this with that which is shadow.

Heb. 10::1 "For the Law, since it has only a shadow of the good things to come and not the very form of things, can never, by the same sacrifices which they offer continually year by year, make perfect those who draw near." NAS.

Not only is the law a shadow, but the temple and tabernacle layout are shadows of our increasing intimacy with the Lord as we grow.

Shadows provide benefits. There is shade or protection provided, but the shadow is not the object providing the shade or protection. There are many shadows in scripture, but the reality of them is bound up in Jesus Christ.

Our ideals are like shadows. Even as the Israelites worshipped their shadows, their ideas of what He would be like when He came. So do we. When He shows up in our lives, we do not recognize Him because our ideals about Him have blinded us. If He causes the loss of these ideals, we are not losing something real, but they are important to us. We have trusted in these rather than God and we experience catastrophic suffering to lose them. They are our lives, our identity, that by which we guide life.

We are like the man in Jeremiah 17:5 *"Cursed is the man who trusts in man, who depends on flesh for his strength, and whose heart turns away from the Lord."* We, the bride, have trusted in ourselves and our ideals rather than the Lord. We have depended upon our own flesh for strength, or upon the flesh of others who seem to live up to our ideal.

Jeremiah 17: 1-2 says," Judah's sin is engraved with an iron tool, inscribed with a flint point, on the tablets of their hearts and on the horns of their altars. Even their children remember their altars and their Ashram poles..."

These ideals are inscribed upon our hearts. We worship our ideas. They are upon the horns of our altars. They are our idols, and our sin affects our children. Our ideals have become theirs. Our gods are their gods. No wonder we are cursed if we trust in man.

When we have this attitude, we trust the wrong people and they hurt us. We trust them because they appear to live up to our ideal. No one can live up to that, so they disappoint us, and they hurt us. They are the reason we are in the tomb. In all honesty, we are the reason, too. Our ideals demanded that death come. Lying there in that tomb, we want to blame everyone who has hurt us. We have no one to blame but ourselves.

This entire process brings us into *Jeremiah 17:7 "But blessed is the man who trusts in the Lord, whose confidence is in Him. He will be like a tree planted by the water that sends out its roots by the stream. It does not fear when heat comes; it has no worries in a year of drought and never fails to bear fruit."* Before, the bride's confidence was in her ideals, her ideas of God. Now lying in the tomb, these are dead, and she is in the first stage of learning to trust God. When she has learned the lessons that come with the tomb and resurrection, she will no longer fear trial. Drought and difficulty in her life will not throw her because she no longer worships her ideas about God. She worships only God, and that sustains her during drought. He is the stream next to which she is planted. No longer planted by the streams of men's ideologies, she thrives no matter what the circumstances.

How can the tomb come after the Banquet of Wine? It is simple. All the wonderful happenings in this book bring a further revelation of **His** cross. That sounds glorious, but it is death dealing when she carries so much with her that must die.

In fact, though she realized at some level His commitment to her, she does not understand the depth of it yet. The circumstances of her life are the arena in which she learns. She understands His covenant in blood, the giving of His life for her, only when she must give up all. The banquet of wine becomes real rather than abstract, only at the loss of everything. Suffering was not something solicited. Recognition of His table causes death in her. This seeing is not the pulling back of a veil while she sits at ease. Rather, it forces her eyes to see during difficulty. Even unbelievers understand that difficulty is the greatest teacher.

Spring and Resurrection

Song 2:8-9a "Listen! My lover! Look! Here he comes, leaping across the mountains, bounding over the hills. My lover is like a gazelle or a young stag."

Now she hears Him. Years in the tomb she has waited upon this day. Years of dead ministry and expectation have given way to His coming. Listen literally means, the voice of my lover. He comes to her by His voice, and she knows He has come to speak to her.

Then she sees Him. *"Look! Here he comes."* But he comes leaping as a gazelle or a young stag. The word gazelle means beauty or glory, and a young stag has strength and sure-footedness. When she sees Him this time, she sees not only His ability to scale the mountains of difficulty, but she also sees His glory. It is His glory, which He won back through suffering (John 17:4-5), that makes Him sure-footed in difficult terrain. He has come to let her know He can scale any difficulty that may come.

Song 2:9b "Look! There he stands behind our wall, gazing through the windows, peering through the lattice."

He is standing behind a wall that belongs to them, gazing through the windows in the wall and peering through a lattice.

This speaks of Him being partially obscured from her vision. The wall is our wall. This is her past. Years in the tomb lessened some pain. Answers were sorted out there. However, like the disciples after Jesus' death, confusion is more the order of the day since only in resurrection will become clear. During her time in the tomb, He reveals His death, burial and resurrection in an extra dimension. The tomb brings the death of all she believes about that, too. Then He replaces the things that were in error with His truth. This takes place during the tomb time and as she comes forth from it. Until that happens, the wall she built between them still exists. He was with her as she built it, but the wall must disappear. One day, her past will have no power over her. Yet now her past still obscures Him somewhat.

If she has yielded to the healing of her soul, then limited ministry takes place, but she knows the depth of suffering often determines the depth of ministry. Indeed, her ministry and her suffering do not match. She knows deep inside that the things she has learned are beyond precious. Over the years, she shared them so little she does not remember their depth. They are obscured behind the lattice with Him. But He knows their value. Resurrection happens in His time and in His way.

Song 2:10 'My lover spoke and said to me, "Arise my darling, my beautiful one and come with me. See! The winter is past, the rains are over and gone. Flowers appear on the earth, the season of singing has come, the cooing of doves is heard in our land."'

Though the past obscures Him from her, she hears His voice. He is saying arise, which shows she is resting. Because the past obscures Him, He reassures her that winter ended. He wants her to come forth from the tomb and go with Him. The time in the tomb is the winter when everything appears dead. His words reassure her that winter is at an end.

This is a hard decision for the bride. Because of this, He is directing her eyes to present realities, not to the future. Hope for the future may be dead within her if He has not yet healed her heart. Even to hear the word future may cause dread that it will be as difficult as before. So, He speaks only of the winter being past and His desire for her to come with Him.

Spring

There are many of his children that never leave slavery. Likewise, others never leave the tomb. The suffering may have embittered them because the church did not teach them what it was about, or they did not understand. They will not emerge because their ideals have deceived them. When the Lord comes to them, they ignore Him because all they can see is the wall of the past. They love Him, but they cannot go on in this life to know Him more intimately. Indeed, the price is too high. They have not only counted the cost; they made it the focus of their life. With their eyes directed toward the price they never see where He will take them. Only with our eyes fixed upon Him and fullness of relationship with Him will we be able to arise. Some will delay until a future time.

To obey and go with Him is to focus on His glory in the earth. The one who says yes wants glory of God to show from their life and any ministry future ministry. His glory is the focus of the eyes and heart. Her ear is tuned to His voice.

To obey and go with Him is to adopt His priorities as our priorities, His will as our will, and His life as our life. This exchanges our life for His. This is the reason for the suffering. *Gal. 2:20 "I have been crucified with Christ and I no longer live, but Christ lives in me. The life I live in the body, I live by faith in the Son of God, who loved me and gave himself for me."* This is one of the glorious purposes of suffering, to become like Him, to make His will our will.

Song 2:13 'The fig tree forms its early fruit; the blossoming vines spread their fragrance. "Arise my darling, my beautiful one, come with me."'

He speaks to her of the fruit growing in her life. Her major thought while He has been speaking was, "Where are you taking me?" The places where they visited before were so hard that fear has gripped her heart. That is why He speaks of fruit. She has been dead, fruitless. He tells her that fruit is now available, but more than that, He tells her again to arise and come with Him. He won't tell her where He is going, only that she is to come **with Him**. All fear aside, she must arise because more than anything else she wants Him. Love for Him is the only reason to arise for those who accept resurrection.

If the bride wants her own way, her own comfort, more than she wants Him, she may never arise. There is one reason enabling her to go on. She wants to know and love Him more than she wants anything.

> *"Arise my darling, my beautiful one, and come with me."*

> " Where are you going Lord?"

> *"Arise my darling, my beautiful one, and come with me."*

> "I will arise."

For Reflection

1. What expectations of God and how the church and ministry work died or need to die?

2. Are you living by the tree of knowledge? In the future, how would you live from the tree of life and love?

3. How much of your past is guided by fear of exposure and shame? Ask the Lord for help. What scripture can you stand in to overcome this fear? Some possibilities would be Lu. 12:3-5, Ps. 71:1, Ps. 71:3, Ps.25.2.

4. Do you ever turn others into objects, so you can speak about them negatively? Is this what happened to you?

5. If you are a woman, were you shamed because of being female? Ask Him to help you get free from the shame of being a woman with a passion for Him.

6. What idolatry do you take part in because of shame?

7. Will you commit to be made ready for the Bridegroom?

8. What ideals and shadows do you look for instead of the real? Who have you trusted in rather than the Lord? Our gods will shame us. What gods were involved in this?

Prayer

Lord Help! I have been an idolater worshipping what I thought was you, but I was worshipping my ideas about you and the way this Christian life works. Set me free from all idolatry, from all my ideas about you. I want you alone. Forgive those who have wounded me. I thank you for them because I needed them to help me die to those things that kept me from you. Be Lord in my life.

Set me free from fear and shame. Show me the path to allow you to be my shield instead of my behaviors shielding me. Help me embrace the tree of life in faith that you are enough. Prepare me as your bride. Give me the fine linen to wear. Help me walk righteously before you. I want to walk as you walked obeying the Father's will. Help me find you in the Secret Place of your presence.

Bring me into confidence in what you purchased for me on Calvary. Retrain my mind to think your thoughts. Plant your seed deep within me and may it bring forth 100-fold, to proclaim your glory in the earth.

Chapter 11

The Voice

He Desires Her Voice

Song 2:14 *"My dove in the clefts of the rock, in the hiding places of the mountainside, show me your face, let me hear your voice; for your voice is sweet, and your face is lovely."*

In leaving the tomb He is calling us to the clefts of the rock. He is the rock or stronghold. When God formed Eve, He took her from Adam's side. Jesus' death birthed the bride. As the spear pierced His side, blood and water gushed out, showing he died of heart failure. Our sin and the crucifixion's agony were too much for his great heart to bear. When His heart ceased to beat, the bride came forth. The sword that pierced his side showed that beginning for the wife of the second Adam.

He was cleft for us, and in Him we are to hide. He calls to His bride to find refuge in Him. Then more, He calls us to the hiding places of the mountainside. The word mountainside refers to a steep place, like a mountain, that needs to be climbed using steps or stairs. Stairs suggest different levels of intimacy and relationship. Remember the chambers of Chapter One? She comes into new chambers, additional steps on the mountain. This means that there will be extra levels of difficulty. Mountains take effort to climb. But He guides her. He will help her understand the great sacrifice He made, what it meant to be the rock that was cleft for her.

He desires to hear her voice and see her face. Therefore, face-to-face fellowship is His desire for two reasons. The first, He loves her and wants to be with her. The second reason is that she will not become whole aside from being in His presence. His voice stills whatever power the voices of the past have over her. His voice instructs her to trust Him. When she fears, and runs to Him, He shows her the truth that renders powerless the lie that causes her to fear.

We are beautiful to Him. He desires us. He desires you. How could He not since He gave up everything to marry us/you? We are His. Yet often we ignore Him. We do not run to Him to be with Him. Too often we do not discern His heart for us, the love He has for us, love beyond understanding. To comprehend this love, we need to be in His presence.

The Voice Covenant Refused

Like all believers, the nation of Israel struggled with fear. *Exodus 19:5-6 "Now therefore, if you will obey my voice indeed, and keep my covenant, then ye shall be a peculiar treasure unto me above all people: for all the earth is mine: And ye shall be unto me a kingdom of priests, and a holy nation." KJV.*

The Lord told the newly escaped slaves if they obeyed His voice, they will be a peculiar treasure, a kingdom of priests and a holy nation. The original Hebrew includes the word voice. This is an important distinction. These three things they did not receive were contingent upon obeying His voice. These three promises were the most important words spoken to the Israelites. So, what happened?

Exodus 20 verses 1-17 begin the story. God spoke the Ten Commandments from Mount Sinai. He did not write them on tablets of stone till later. He wanted to write them on men's hearts as they listened to His voice, as we noticed in Exodus 19. Ex. 20:18 records the Israelite's reaction to His voice.

Exodus 20:18 'When the people saw the thunder and lightning and heard the trumpet and saw the mountain in smoke, they trembled with fear. They stayed at a distance and said to Moses, "Speak to us yourself and we will listen, but do not have God speak to us or we will die. Moses said to the people, "Do not be afraid. God has come to test you so that the fear of God will be with you to keep you from sinning." The people remained at a distance...'

Too often, we respond to God's awesome presence or the mountains of difficulty by remaining at a distance. God offered them a covenant by His voice. Listening and obeying was all they needed to do. They could have admitted their fear, asked for and received courage and pressed in to know God as He spoke to them. Instead, the Israelites retreated from Him in fear. They set aside a proper fear of God. Moreover, they were afraid of the voice, the lightning and the trumpet. They trusted in Moses to hear for them. That was a fatal mistake. Moses was a wise man, but not all their leaders were. Many of those they trusted over the ensuing years led them astray. The same is true of us. Allowing others to listen in our place could stunt our development and potentially lead us astray.

By rejecting this covenant, spoken directly to them by God, , they received a law they could never fulfill. They refused the promise of God to become a peculiar treasure, a kingdom of priests and a holy nation.

1Pet. 2:9 But you are a chosen people, a royal priesthood, a holy nation, a people belonging to God, that you may declare the praises of him who called you out of darkness into his wonderful light.

1Pet. 2:10 "Once you were not a people, but now you are the people of God; once you had not received mercy, but now you have received mercy." This is the Ex. 19 promise now repeated to those who came to the Father through Christ. He freely gives what they refused to all who make Him Lord today.

Consider the words of *Jeremiah 7:22-24* *"For I spake not unto your fathers, nor commanded them in the day that I brought them out of the land of Egypt, concerning burnt offerings or sacrifices: But this thing commanded I them, saying, Obey my voice, and I will be your God, and you shall be my people: and walk ye in all the ways that I have commanded you that it may be well unto you. But they hearkened not, nor inclined their ear, but walked in the counsels and in the imagination of their evil heart and went backward and not forward." KJV.*

His original command did not concern sacrifices and offerings, but listening to and obeying His voice. Instead, they walked in the counsels of their imagination. They did not cast down the past voices. They did not take captive those slave voices of Egypt. Yes, they were afraid of His glory on the mountain, but their problem went deeper than that. They knew slavery but did not know God. The imaginations of their hearts were familiar. Hebrews says they had a fearful and unbelieving heart (Hebrews 3:12). Fear kept them from trusting in God. At the mountain, they refused to hear Him because of fear and unbelief.

The Voice Covenant Through Christ

The bride must come close to Him and find refuge in the one cleft for her, so she can hear His voice. His voice will put to flight every vestige of fear as she learns to dwell in His presence.

This is hard. You have heard the voice of the enemy telling you what it tells her. "Others hear the voice of God, but not you. You are not as worthy to hear Him. You don't hear well; face it. Your sin separates you from His voice." These are lies. We are adept at discerning the lies. If these voices reach us, we also can hear Him. At Sinai, He came to set up a covenant by His voice. The former slaves refused it. At Calvary, He reestablished the covenant, signing it in His own blood. He cared enough for that covenant by voice to die to establish it.

Our bride is listening for His voice and understands His love more deeply.

Song 2:16 "My lover is mine and I am his; he browses among the lilies."

The bride's understanding of their relationship still misses the point. Though she understands more than before, not until the end of Song of Songs in Chapter 7 does she feel secure in His love. For now, she rejoices He is hers and she is His. She cannot comprehend more than this yet. Many more experiences must come before she can understand the depth of the love He offers.

He browses among the lilies. This must be the lilies that are among the thorns, His bride. Her understanding of His love is more general than it will one day be. The Bridegroom's love goes so far beyond the statement, "My lover is mine and I am his." Romantic love, with its false ideals, makes that declaration. We love only because He first loved us. Relationship with Him is based on His all-encompassing love, not our possession of Him. Maturity will teach her this. For now, she rejoices in the romantic excitement. For now, she sees Him among the lilies, His people. She is not yet ready to experience the fullness of His love. One day she will know. Now she cannot guess there is more.

> It will take more darkness.
> It will take the nearness of true communion.
> It will take hearing His voice
> without reservation.
> It will take till the end of His song.

For Reflection

1. What sacrifices and offerings do you offer Him in the place of "face to face" intimate communion?

2. What fears keep you in unbelief? Cry out to Him with each one and ask Him to show you how to fight them. Write done the plan and review it often.

3. What lies keep you from knowing His great love for you?

4. What lies do you believe that keep you from hearing His voice?

5. Is there someone that you expect to be the voice of God to you? How will you allow God to speak instead?

Prayer

Lord, help me know how much I need you. Heal my blindness and cause my spiritual eyes to be fixed on you. Have mercy on me and heal me of the fears that keep me worshipping other gods. Speak to me, for I belong to you; help me know I belong. Let your words change me. Let them wound me and heal me and make me yours.

Chapter 12

Separation

Let the Shadows Flee

Song *2:17 "Until the day breaks and the shadows flee, turn my lover and be like a gazelle or a young stag on the rugged hills."*

This passage describes the reply of the bride if she decides not to stay in the tomb. If we feel the price so far is too high, we may reply that we will stay where we are until the day breaks and the shadows flee. His call to come forth because spring has arrived may not be enough.

For those that heeded His call to arise, our bride has come through a sweet time in the Lord's presence, although short. Yes, short. For next she faces a time of separation. She is human and therefore flawed. Those flaws sometimes separate. This is like the tomb. He is gone from her, and night has fallen, *"Until the day breaks and the shadows flee"*. The bride speaks of Him as a gazelle or young stag on the hills as she did when He came to announce the end of winter, the end of the tomb. She recognizes the day will one-day break. Separation is hard, but the tomb's bitterness is not in this. The despair is gone because resurrection has shown her that His presence will be available again someday.

The Desperate Dream

Song 3:1 "All night long on my bed, I looked for the one my heart loves; I looked for him but did not find him."

She is looking, musing in her mind and dreaming while lying on her bed. The bride is resting from her difficulties. She wants life to be "normal," this means easy. Life should be uncomplicated, as life is for believers that will not seek His presence. This shows she is not yet desperate for His presence. She has taken Him for granted. If she will find Him, she must pursue Him. Desperation for Him must grow in her heart. The Bible tells us if we seek Him, we will find Him, but we must seek Him with our whole heart. (Jeremiah 29:12) She seeks Him while in a dream state, lying on her bed. Only after time passed without Him does she get desperate. Night means a time of difficulty. Since she believes that life should be normal, it was difficult for her to realize that she must do more than rest.

Song 3:2 "I will get up now and go about the city, through its streets and squares; I will search for the one my heart loves. So, I looked for him but did not find him."

When He has been absent long enough, she gets up from her complacent resting place to look for Him. She goes through the city's streets and squares. The squares are the places where the leaders do business, and the streets signify the common man. She is going to anyone who helps her find Him. She is again looking to man. Therefore, the result of this is, *"I looked for him but did not find him."* The Lord is calling her to intimacy with Him. Others cannot hear God for her if she is to grow to the maturity that will ready her for the marriage.

Song 3:3 "The watchmen found me as they made their rounds in the city. 'Have you seen the one my heart loves?' Scarcely had I passed them when I found the one my heart loves. I held him and would not let him go, till I had brought him to my mother's house, to the room of the one who conceived me."

Next the watchmen found her. Even they could not help her. It was not until she passed them that she found Him. Though the church watchmen church should know where He is and the enemy's danger, they often do not. Throughout the years of Israel's history and now church history, the watchmen prophets often prophesied what the leaders of the nation wanted to hear. They were not true watchmen, but full of self-interest, prophesying for pay, recognition, or love of power. There were few watchmen who carried a genuine message. The Isaiah's, Jeremiah's and Ezekiel's were the exceptions. A similar situation exists today. These watchmen cannot help her. Indeed, she must find Him for herself.

It is in passing the watchmen she finds Him. This is a lesson she must learn. Anyone who wants to know Him as He is must learn to seek Him without the help of others. In fact, God uses others to speak to us, but that only complements that which the Lord is building in us.

This experience has caused her to love and desire Him more. She held Him and would not let Him go. She never wants to lose Him again. The time without Him has deepened her love. We fickle humans need to be without His benefits, so we might miss them. Then when we receive them back, we can appreciate them.

Not only did she not want to let Him go, but she brought Him to her mother's room. It is not clear here if this passage speaks of her mother, the church, or her mother humanity. What is clear, however, is she wants to share Him with others. Whether saved or unsaved, she must bring Him to others. She wants to share how much she loves Him and how glad she is to have Him back. His absence is a necessary part of the bride's growth and a normal consequence of her actions.

Song 3:5 "Daughters of Jerusalem, I charge you by the gazelles and by the doses of the field: Do not arouse or awaken love until it so desires."

Again, she instructs the others in the church not to force the love that is growing in her heart. Awakening to love happens as the Lord loves and draws His bride. There is love to be awakened. She will have times where she rests when He is calling her. He is infinitely patient, waiting for the love of His bride.

The tomb held her, but now His love holds her.

Only He loves so well love awakens.

Only He died so love was possible.

Only He....

For Reflection

1. Do you desire a normal life?
2. How do you define normal? If you compare the radical life our savior lived, what are the differences?
3. What wounds of your past do you need to understand from God's point of view? What is He saying to you about the wounds? Go before Him with your bible and listen, write what He is saying. Continue to do this over the years until you have His mind on your experiences and you are healed according to His plan.
4. How can you embrace the radical path He has for you? Ask Him to show you and write what He is saying.

Prayer

Lord, help me see you and to quit looking at past hurt and challenges except to allow them to train me in what is real in your kingdom. Show me who you are in such a way it changes my life forever. Help me think like you. Forgive me for wanting a "normal" life. You are the only answer I need, but often I want other answers. Do the work in me that needs to be done to bring my thoughts in alignment with yours. Empower me to do my part

Chapter 13
The Wedding Procession

Tomb Lessons

These next two chapters illustrate lessons learned while our bride was in the tomb. We bewail our fate until we realize what He has done for us, until we see the depth of His love, a love that is measureless. The purpose for difficulty is that she might enter a new depth of love relationship with the Bridegroom. This occurs in the believer when they experience chapter three and four of Song of Songs. He draws each believer into intimacy of fellowship like marriage. This relationship is spiritual. But the spiritual relationship is like the closeness of the physical relationship in marriage. He wants to be the object of her passion. Too often in the past ministry, or pleasing men was the object of her passion. She gave her time and effort to the seeking of many things. When the bride lives reality of these third and fourth chapters of Song of Songs, she leaves behind the tendency to let these other selfish motives drive her life.

Now I want to tell you, my story. It is the story of love rather than slavery and persecution. When I got married, I thought I had chosen a rather ordinary man. In fact, the Lord chose him for me, and had to teach me to love him. I married a most extraordinary man, but as a widow of only 6 months, it took many years to realize it. That is just like our bride. Many years pass before she realizes how wonderful the Bridegroom is. Trial taught me what a prize my husband was. No matter how much I hurt my husband, how willful I was, or how little I regarded his advice, he loved me. I was un-submissive, controlling, angry, selfish, a religious addict, a victim in constant crisis, like our bride, and he loved me. He let me fail and learn. He did not dictate. When people trampled me because of the sickness in my life, he picked up the pieces and loved me despite my neurosis. His love strengthened me. I could not help but love him in return. Being loved so well, I learned to submit. I came to see the controlling tendencies in my life for the sickness they were. It became impossible to control someone who loved so well. Because of love, I saw my religious addiction and the fear of man that drove me to be a victim. I worked to get well for my husband because of his love. I also wanted to be well for my children, and, most of all, for my Heavenly Bridegroom because of love.

My husband in the natural fulfilled the role of my spiritual husband until I understood. In fact, I cannot tell you when it was the love of my husband or the love of the Bridegroom that ministered to me, for it was the love of the Bridegroom through my husband I experienced. My husband was a living epistle of the Lord's love. We have living epistles in our lives that exhibit the love of God and help us through the hard times. Sometimes one is a good friend or could be a family member, but their love demonstrates the love of the Bridegroom to us and helps us continue without quitting.

What my husband did, the Lord does for us. He loves us through all our sins. That love, amid our mess, gets through to us. It is always and ever His love that brings any healing in our lives. He is more committed to us than we know. We can never understand how much he loves us. He reveals that love during pain because of so much wreckage and sin in our lives. It is not because He enjoys seeing us suffer. The wonder is that in that wreckage and sin, He loves us with abandon and to the full extent of His love, a love that has no end.

On the Way to Calvary

These next two chapters in His Song will draw us in to a newness of intimacy with Him. The love we understand after experiencing the reality of these chapters will be so much more than we understood. Notice I did not say we would understand after reading these chapters, but after experiencing the reality of them. That means we must enter the reality of what these chapters mean, leaving behind the shadow, the ideal of intimacy we have had. In a healthy marriage love grows deeper as the years pass. Each partner becomes more in tune with the other, and love grows. This is true with Him and true in my marriage. In my case, I was the one who loved little and had barriers against love, just as the bride does. My husband had no barriers, even as the Lord has none. The Lord cannot have barriers because He is Love.

I Corinthians 13 tells us *"love is patient"*. He is patient while He draws us and loves us beyond our ability to understand.

Song 3:6 "Who is this coming up from the desert like a column of smoke, perfumed with myrrh and incense made from all the spices of the merchant?"

The word for desert refers to land useable only for pasture, or a dry, solitary region. It is an isolated place. The word isolated means to be separated or to obtain purity. The Lord came from a separated place of purification. Satan tempted Him after a forty-day fast in the desert and Jesus triumphed. (Matt. 4:1-10)

God prepared Moses through forty years in the desert. The Israelites failed in the desert. Since the Son succeeded in the desert, we know it is possible to succeed there. We obey and believe God through Him. He came from a place of separation unto the Father and obedience to His will when He married the bride.

The word column is used nowhere else in scripture, but the word smoke is the same as in *Isaiah 4:5. "Then the Lord will* create over all of Mount Zion and over all those who assemble there a cloud of smoke by day and a glow of flaming fire by night." This smoke is significant of the glory of God. When the High Priest entered the Holy of Holies on the Day of Atonement, he took incense with him to offer at the mercy seat of the Ark of God's Presence until the cloud of incense covered it. The Lord was the incense offered before the Father on the Day of Atonement.

Psalm 45:8 "All of your garments are fragrant with myrrh, aloes, and cassia." Psa. 45 is another picture of the Lord as the incense. Here incense is upon His royal robes on His wedding day. Incense is a type of His attributes and a type of prayer. Only as prayer covered the mercy seat could the High Priest be accepted. The Lord interceded for us at Calvary and He ever lives to make intercession for us.

We see His attributes in the myrrh and frankincense of the incense. Myrrh is an ingredient of the anointing oil and holy incense (EX. 30). In the same way as He was scourged for us, the bark of the myrrh tree had to be scored, so the sap seeped out and hardened. It was then ground to powder for the incense. Myrrh was an embalming spice.[xiv] This pictures what happens next. He died to marry His bride.

Frankincense was part of the holy incense. It was white when in its purest form and white means purity. This, too, speaks of His separation. It fixed the odor of the mixture, so it will last. This death He died was once for all. It lasts for eternity. The Wise Men gave Him myrrh and frankincense [xv] at His birth, signifying not only His death, but further, His marriage through the giving of His life.

They gathered both myrrh and frankincense [xvi] in wilderness areas. Likewise, the Father perfected Him in the wilderness of suffering. He perfects us there as well. Psalm 45 is a wedding song. Verse 8 says, "All your robes are fragrant with myrrh and aloes and cassia." The fragrance He is becomes ours as our bark is scored in the wilderness of suffering. Then that fragrance fills the earth.

2Corinthians 2:15 "For we are to God the aroma of Christ among those who are being saved and those who are perishing."

To be the fragrance of Christ, we must walk as He walked. He learned obedience through suffering. We cannot become as He is by taking the path of least resistance. His suffering is the path to the fragrance.

Song 3:7 "Look! It is Solomon's carriage, escorted by sixty warriors, the noblest of Israel, all of them wearing the sword, all experienced in battle, each with his sword at his side, prepared for the terrors of the night."

Our heavenly Solomon is coming in procession. He is in the bridal carriage, as we shall see later. Warriors with swords surround Him. These are the saints that stand in the front lines that His presence comes into His bride. Likewise, just before His betrayal, Jesus told His disciples that if they did not have a sword, they should buy one because many consider Him a transgressor, *Luke 22:36.* Throughout the ages there have been those warriors that lay down their lives literally and in prayer that the purposes of God may go forth. These warriors signify the warfare we will take part in if we accept this covenant in His blood.

Sixty warriors prepared for the terrors of the night. Our Bridegroom embraced the terrors of the night of Calvary in this passage. Warriors in His kingdom must be battle ready and willing to die.

Revelation 12:11 "They overcame him by the blood of the lamb, and the word of their testimony, and they loved not their lives so much as to shrink from death."

This dying process is a fearful thing to us because we must lay aside the things of this world that hold our hearts and accept a life in Christ that we have yet to master. When the enemy whispers that the Lord couldn't love us because life is so hard, and our circumstances prove we are alone, we slay that lie. This brings further death to fear, bondage, and our selfishness. Every time we experience the reality of the cross at work in our lives more fear dies, and we become more alive to God.

The setting of this passage is Calvary, the Holy of Holies, and the sacrifice of Passover. Song of Songs is read at the Passover. He was the Passover Lamb.

The Ultimate Volunteer
Song *3:9 "King Solomon made for himself the carriage..."*

This means, *"I lay down my life.... No one takes it from me, I lay it down of my own accord."* (John 10:17-18) He has a conveyance which carries Him to His bride. He built this carriage for Himself by laying down His life. He was a volunteer unto death. The bride of His heart could only be obtained through death.

Song 9b-10 "he made it of wood from Lebanon. Its posts he made of silver, its base he made of gold, its seat was upholstered with purple, its interior lovingly inlaid by the daughters of Jerusalem."

The wood from Lebanon is the cedar. That is a type of His sinless humanity. No worm or corruption could feed on the wood. This was the major component of His bridal carriage. Without His sinless humanity, there would be no wedding, no atonement. All else is built upon that truth.

The posts hold up a canopy. Posts are for strength and support. These silver posts signify our redemption. On the Day of Atonement, a silver coin made atonement for the people.

The base of gold is a type of the mercy seat *Ex. 25:1*. On the Day of Atonement the High Priest entered the Holy of Holies and made atonement for the entire nation. The glory of the Lord appeared over the mercy seat. Earlier we saw Him as the incense over the mercy seat. He is the incense and the Glory. The Glory appeared over the mercy seat in the bridal carriage on the way to Calvary. This is easy to understand since every offering of the temple speaks of Him. This gold base is significant of His perfection. We place everything else upon that perfection.

The purple covering the seat is a sign of royalty and one color in the veil of the temple *Ex. 26:31-33*. Those who yearn for the bridegroom lovingly inlaid the interior.

The wedding procession that day traveled the Via Dolorosa, the way of the cross. Solomon got to ride in the marvelous conveyance described in the above passage. In contrast, our Heavenly Solomon carried a cross to His wedding. His garments were fragrant with the smell of His own blood until they removed them from Him and nailed His tortured, bloody body to the cross He carried to Golgotha. He was the fragrance of sacrifice that was acceptable.

His Crown

Song 3:11 *"Come out you daughters of Zion, and look at King Solomon wearing the crown, the crown with which his mother crowned him on the day of his wedding..."*

Before the daughters were called daughters of Jerusalem. Now they are daughters of Zion. Zion is the place of God's presence. Zion is the church birthed through His death. The verbs in this passage are past tense, as if the crucifixion has occurred.

We daughters of Zion are told to come see the crown that His mother used to crown Him. This is the crown given by His mother humanity. Humanity crowned Him with a crown of thorns. The only crown we could give Him was one that mocked His Godhood, but, one day we will give Him crowns. Scripture shows the believer receiving crowns of life, glory and righteousness *(James 1:12, Rev. 2:10, 1Pet 5:4, 2 Tim. 4:8)*. *Revelation 4:10* shows the twenty-four elders casting their crowns before the Lamb. In glory, we will cast our crowns before Him and that is possible because one day, He wore our crown of thorns.

We are told that the day of His wedding was *"the day his heart rejoiced", Song 3:11b.* How does his heart rejoice at crucifixion? *Hebrews 12:2 "For the joy set before him, he endured the cross...."* The joy set before Him was His bride. This joy enabled Him to lie down His life. His love for us is immense, and we can persevere through anything for the joy that awaits us. What is more, the joy is a relationship with Him.

He makes this more real to the Bride only as she dies to her ideas, so she can see His sacrifice and love well. Although she does not realize it, the death and tomb strip away the false and begin replacing it with the real.

A Life for a Life

A life for a life
Oh, bloody sacrifice.

To purchase me
through tortured tree,
but more
to marry me
through life out poured
is wonder beyond wonder

Hear, Oh heart
and love
and finally love.

For Reflection

1. What in the world holds your heart and keeps you from the battle for your own life and loved ones?

2. In what ways do you "shrink from death" and love your own life too much?

3. How can you move from the crown of thorns you placed on Him to crowns of life, glory and righteous-ness for you?

4. How can you move into a new level of warfare through your new understanding?

5. Are you willing to allow your own death to self to do warfare on behalf of others?

Prayer

Lord, I read this account of your death and I am undone. How can you desire me? How can the mess I call a life be the joy set before you? I am told that as Song of Song unfolds, this answer is within the pages. But I know what I am. I so much want to glorify you with my life. I struggle with seeing this glory is possible.

Help me be willing day by day to give up the things that hold my heart and my flesh and keep me from your fullness. Lord, you deserve everything. Forgive me for giving you so little and draw me into the place of total dedication to you. Show me what it means to be your bride, so I desire you more than anything in this life.

Four out of seven books. To see more or learn about the author click the first link below.

http://www.amazon.com/author/debrawebster

To go to the website click the link below.
https://bridesheart.com

The Joy Set Before Him

His Joy

If troubled fellowships are your history, this next concept may be hard for you to accept. If you have been in complacent fellowships, you may not care. However, if you are at the right place in your journey, then this may change forever your understanding of His love.

Whether you can relate to this, we were the joy, He viewed when He endured the cross. Even if you do not believe it or do not care, we were.

Let's make this personal. You were the joy before Him as He died on Calvary. That is remarkable. You and all those flawed humans you fellowship with were His joy. Because of you, Calvary was worth it.

This passage describes the joy set before Him. It describes His bride, you. It is also the song the Bridegroom sang in praise of His bride on their wedding day. This was an eastern custom. The day He died, the description that follows was singing in His heart as He viewed His bride, as He viewed you.

The description that follows is imperative to growth in intimacy. Scripture tells us we love because He first loved us. That is not just true in salvation, but also in the growth of intimacy. As He shows His love to us, we grow in love. This is a constant process.

Think of where our bride has been. Recently, she was a slave because she needed men's approval. Slaves lack love. In fact, the lack of love made her willing to be enslaved. When the Lord comes to us as Bridegroom, He comes to reveal His love.

The bride needed the revelation of His death provided in the last chapter, so she hears of His love for her in this one. That shows us we cannot understand Him unless we keep His cross central.

Hebrews 2:12 "Let us fix our eyes upon Jesus, the author and perfecter of our faith, who for the joy set before him endured the cross, scorning its shame, and sat down at the right hand of the throne of God."

Not only were we His joy, but we are told to fix our eyes upon Him. We are to allow Him to be our joy when we face death of self. He has not called us to carry our cross without hope. He is our joy and our hope on the way to our personal Calvary.

Your Focus

Hebrews *12:3 "Consider Him who endured such opposition from sinful men, so that you will not grow weary and lose heart."* As we consider Him, our focus is upon His cross. That focus shows His delight in us, and His love for us. That gives us encouragement to take up our cross daily.

So many failures today are because we made our teachings the focus rather than the cross. It is the Lamb to whom we must point in all we preach and teach. He must be the focus of leaders and the people, not building man-made ministries and kingdoms. Many worship success as god, setting aside a focus upon the Lord. When man's vision becomes the focus of a work, the people worship the man and the vision. When we do this, we think we are still worshipping God. The focus is off God and onto what we can do. We become men who worship men. It does not take the New Age movement to worship self as god. It happens regularly in our churches.

This brings much loss to the Lord's people. Intimacy requires a focus on the Lord. Without the Lamb central to all, we cannot hear what is about to be spoken by the Bridegroom.

The Lord cannot draw into intimacy those who refuse to be drawn. Those who hide from the truth about the relationship games they play refuse intimacy. In fact, playing games of power, superiority, domination, popularity and living in denial and deception keep the believer from entering the intimacy that the Lord died to provide.

He yearns to speak face to face with each believer. He desires to make us His. This is pain's purpose. It is not to fulfill the capriciousness of a vengeful God. Losing the false ideas, we trust in brings pain. It is even more painful to hang onto the false. Yielding to God brings life. Yielding to the false brings more and more pain, like a snowball rolling down a hill. Or if we are adept at hiding from the pain, then we may become a source of great pain and hurt to others. Those who deny pain often become autocratic persecutors. Either way, holding on to the false is a losing proposition. Only in surrender to His love will we find wholeness.

Separation Unto Him

Song *4:1 "How beautiful you are my darling! Oh, how beautiful! Your eyes behind your veil are doves."*

She is no longer a man pleaser. Transformation has changed her from likeness to the daughters of Zion mentioned in Isaiah 3:16 "...haughty, with outstretched necks, flirting with their eyes." Once she was a flirt, but many trials taught her where to keep her eyes. She is instead like the prophet Isaiah. Isaiah 6:1 In the year that King Uzziah died, I saw the Lord." The other delights that would hold her attention are dead to her. Like Isaiah she sees only Him. Her dove's eyes make her beautiful to Him.

The word beautiful in this passage means bright. Those who see the Holiness of God as Isaiah did, carry His brightness on their countenance. Indeed, even as the glory of God brought purging to Isaiah's life, it brings purging to the life of all who behold Him. He overshadows His bride with the glory of God amid many trials and it shows.

Matthew 6:22-23 "The eye is the lamp of the body, if your eyes are good, your whole body will be full of light. But if your eyes are bad, your whole body will be full of darkness. If then the light that is within you is darkness, how great is the darkness."

The bride's eyes are full of light. That the light within is darkness suggests what is considered light is not light but deception instead. The bride is coming out of deception by others and no longer lives in self-deception. Deception and self-deception were in her life as a slave. They were in her life in the tomb. In that tomb love for them died. In the tomb her eyes became dove's eyes. Though she is sometimes tempted to win the praise of men, she is quick to repent when she succumbs to the charms of men rather than the Lord.

She set her heart to love and know the Lord. She lost her expectations of ministry and success. In fact, these do not matter to her anymore. She only wants to succeed in His eyes and that means, as the word of our wedding vows go, "Forsaking all others."

Song 4:1b "Your hair is like a flock of goats descending from Mount Gilead."

Mount Gilead is shaped like the head and shoulders of a man. When the black goats graze on the mountainside, it looks like it is covered with hair. Long hair is a symbol of separation and subjection. The Nazirite separated himself unto God all the days of his vow and was not to cut his hair. Not only did long hair indicate separation in the Old Testament, but in the New Testament, a woman's hair was her covering and signified subjection to her husband.

The bride is separated unto and submissive to God. She does not make an outward show of submission to impress others, but she delights to do His will. However, there are those who know how to look submissive through quoting scripture and posturing while all the time manipulating everyone that comes within their sphere. They are clever; able to convince people they are holy. They can deceive those who worship men. The bride used to believe them until she woke up and saw she was their slave. The bride knew how to look submissive. She was good at posturing, but no more. The religious exercise of the past died. She is alive unto the will of God.

Song 4:2 "Your teeth are like a flock of sheep just shorn, coming up from the washing. Each has its twin; not one of them is alone."

Can you imagine a man engaged to a woman tell her that her hair is like a flock of goats? Her teeth resemble newly shorn sheep, just brushed, and none are missing. It sounds like a man inspecting a farm animal before buying.

If we were to interpret this passage literally, there would be no other conclusion except, He was inspecting her. The real meaning has nothing to do with inspection. On the other hand, it has everything to do with love.

We use teeth for chewing food. The bride know He is the bread of life and feeds on Him.

Jeremiah 15:16 "When your words came I ate them; they were my joy and my hearts delight, for I bear your name, O Lord God Almighty."

The bride feeds on His words. The words that Jeremiah is speaking of are more than scripture he was reading. It was the word that God was revealing to him. Those words were his joy and his hearts delight because Jeremiah bore His name. To bear His name means to be betrothed. Jeremiah experienced intimate communion with God. He knew what it was to be the bride feasting on the words of God, so he could bear the weight of his calling.

Her teeth are like sheep, newly shorn and washed. Before we shear and wash sheep, they are very dirty and shaggy. Ugly teeth are not taken care of properly. His word makes her teeth strong and beautiful.

These sheep are coming up from the washing. Coming up suggests they were down somewhere. The bride visits the waters of repentance, so she can be cleansed. The process of eating His words always includes repentance. His words uncover the lies of the enemy. The bride does not excuse sin or explain it away; she repents.

"Each has its twin, not one of them is alone." She learned to repent quickly and to feed on His words. This has strengthened her spiritual teeth. None are missing to disfigure her beauty. If she fed on brown sugar Christianity, she would have gaps in her smile. If she listened to the words of men that lack truth, she would have gaps.

Redeemed Speech

Song 4:3 "Your lips are like a scarlet ribbon; your mouth is lovely...."

The bride's lips are scarlet like the blood of Jesus because He cleansed them.

Isaiah 6:5-6 "'Woe to me! I cried. I am a man of unclean lips, and I live among a people of unclean lips, and my eyes have seen the King, the Lord almighty. Then one of the seraphs flew to me with a live coal in his hand, which he had taken with tongs from the altar. With it he touched my mouth and said, "See this has touched your lips; your guilt is taken away and your sin is atoned for."'

She saw the Lord and thereby noticed her sin and cried out against it. He atoned for her sin and purged her lips. They are a scarlet ribbon because of His sacrifice and her repentance.

She can no longer speak whatever she would like but is learning to speak what He approves. *Revelation 14:5 shows the Bride in the symbolism of the 144,000. "No lie was found in their mouth, they were blameless."* There was no lie in their mouth because suffering purged the lie in the heart. These persecuted saints stand for the bride. Her heart is purged of the lie handed down from her forefathers; so, her lips are also clean.

Song 4:3b "Your temples behind your veil are like the halves of a pomegranate."

The pomegranate is a fruit with white and red flesh and red liquid seeds. This speaks of the righteousness and blood of the Lord. The temples are literally the forehead. *Jeremiah 3:3* speaks of Israel having a whore's forehead. The harlot Babylon has a name on her forehead, *"Mystery Babylon the Great the Mother of Prostitutes." (Revelation 17)*

Upon the forehead of the bride, is His righteousness and redemption. These keep her from participating with harlotry and worship of other gods. She has allowed her idols to be smashed. He is all she sees.

Intercessor

Song 4:4 "Your neck is like the tower of David, built with elegance; on it hang a thousand shields, all of them shields of warriors."

This describes a watchtower. The Lord trained her through many trials to recognize the enemy when he approaches. The 1000 warrior's shields speak of intercession too. An intercessor wars against the enemy for the good of God's people. Our bride is experienced in warfare and committed to the perfection of the church. Since the watchmen could not help her find Him, she learned to find Him for herself and is growing into a great warrior, and intercessor or watchman.

Isaiah 62:6 "I have posted watchmen on your walls, O Jerusalem; they will never be silent day or night. You who call on the Lord give yourselves no rest and give him no rest till he establishes Jerusalem and makes her the praise of the earth."

The Intercessor

Silently and hidden, they kneel,
those who battle darkness in the night.
Against powers and principalities, they do war,
knowing only Him who gives the light.

No laurel wreaths in life will they receive,
just on their knees day by day they kneel.
Their ministry, known only to the King,
His heart the only thing that they can feel.

In glory, there waits a crown of gold,
but in this life only His travail.
Men do not give rewards for this,
but God will take them within the veil.

Working for no reward but Him,
lives laid down in supplications deep.
Concerned with His will and heart,
loving not ease nor even sleep.

Broken-hearted for the sin of the church,
That causes bondage yet to remain.
They stand within the gaping gap,
To see the church whole once again.

Broken because the lost are not saved,
seeing it is because we have sinned.
Repenting, dying, resurrected, now they pray,
to see the people set free from their sin.

On they pray their understanding clear,
eternity now within their view.
The Father's heart is the issue here,
at His side stand these chosen few.

Incense on the altar does arise,
prayer ascends now before the throne.
The hand of God moves to stem the tide,
to cause the heathen to become His own.

Yet on their knees they stay,
knowing only this for sure.
It's always time to pray,
the church has yet to be made pure.

Glory of Glories is moving through His church,
no credit will these humble prayers take.
A worthless servant has only done his work,
it was all done only for His sake.

The smile of God to them is enough,
to hear His laughter ring throughout the earth.
His heart delighted as He now does touch,
His love, His bride, His lovely full-grown church.
© Debra L. Webster 1987

Is this difficult? It is what He sees when He looks at her. She is currently learning, even if she hasn't mastered everything yet. The bride has the heart of God for the lost and the saved in increasing measure. The intimacy of fellowship with Him increases her knowledge of His heart and increases the burden of intercession. This brings her into the call that was upon Isaiah. He was a prophet. The bride has a prophet's heart. Since she knows the heart of God, she speaks as He has her speak, and this includes difficult messages. She is obedient to speak the hard word when needed because the souls of men hang in the balance. The bride is prophetic. Prophetic means she hears the voice of God in the Secret Place of His Presence and speaks as

He wills. All God's people should do this. It should not be unusual to be a watchman prophet. It should be the norm.

At one time, she noticed problems and tried to fix them. The result was she took burdens upon herself that were not hers to carry. Then she felt responsible when problems refused to be fixed. Through this she placed herself in the role of a victim. In fact, others likely blamed her for the failure. But she has learned to leave the fixing to God. The true enemy was revealed to her through fellowship with the Bridegroom. She knows the Lord is the only one who wins the victory. Now a warrior rather than a victim, she wars for others according to the will of God and He brings victory.

It is because she knows His heart that she prays. It is not a religious exercise to win the approval of God. True intercession is born out of love. That is why the first step to the consummation is His death. Since His sacrifice for us is part of the marriage ceremony, and His sacrifice causes us to love, it is the beginning point for intercession.

God's Glory in Ministry

Song 4:5 *"Your two breasts are like two fawns, like twin fawns of a gazelle that browse among the lilies."*

The word gazelle means glory. The breasts of ministry and nurturing are full of the glory of God. Isaiah 6:8 'Then I heard the voice of the Lord saying, "Whom shall I send, and who will go for us? "The glory of God and the cleansing that comes from confrontation with the Almighty transformed Isaiah's ministry. We need those who minister transformed by His glory. Not using His glory to look good, but transformed by the Holy Other.

Unless ministry flows out of a confrontation with the Holy, it will have deadly poison mixed in with it. Each believer holds poisonous religious attitudes. As we grow, many of these fall away, but we often pick up new ones along the way. The sure way to shed them is in His presence. Song of Songs shows the way to the life-changing experience. It is most often a continual unveiling during the struggles of our lives. If we want to know Him more than any other thing, then we shall know Him. *Jeremiah 29:12* promises us this.

This section describes the one who was set before Him while He died. Picture the Savior upon the cross. Sinless, tortured, cut off from the Father. There was only one motivating factor that sent Him to that death. Song of Songs Chapter Four describes what He saw while He hung there dying. He saw His bride. Let that truth sink into your soul, and intercession will be born if it has not been already. He saw us the way Song 4 describes us. Not yet perfect, but having the attributes this passage describes. We were not set before Him, as we will be later in the book when we are more mature. The bride He saw was full of potential, learning so many things. He saw her heart for Him. That was His joy.

We Were the Joy
He stood in the judgment hall of men,
sentenced to die, an innocent man.
 We were the joy.

He hung there upon the cross,
blood flowing from head, hands, and feet.
 We were the joy.
His eternal eye saw not the hatred of men
but rather the fidelity of the Bride.
 We were the joy.

We were the reason for the cross.
And we were something else, too.
We were the joy.

For Reflection

1. Tell the Lord what makes it hard for you to see yourself as the bride described in this chapter. Pray through them listening to Him and writing what they are and what He speaks to you.

2. What things keep you from fixing your eyes on Jesus? How can you overcome these?

3. How do you see the Lord developing dove's eyes in you?

4. Do you delight to hear the Lord both in His word and in Him presently speaking? Do you give Him time to speak through both means? If not, what can you change?

Prayer

Lord, teach me how to quit allowing other loves, other gods into my life. Let dove's eyes for you become the reality of my life. Set me free from man pleasing and excusing away my sin. Help me learn to feed on your word and the words you are speaking to me. I no longer want to give myself to the Harlot domain in the earth. Set me free from self-deception and the darkness that lives within me. Let the light within me be light rather than darkness, I call light.

Help me see what you are calling me to, what you saw as you died. Help me desire you more than what this life can offer. I know you have said I am the joy, help me become all you desire. Give me the vision that Isaiah had, whether it comes through the experience of years or in a moment. Help me see your glory, holiness, love, and forgiveness. Set me free from those things that hold my heart. Make me beautiful with your beauty, holy with your holiness and may I reflect your glory without distortion.

Bridegroom Lamb, I want to understand your sacrifice, not only on the day you died, but throughout your life. You became a man and suffered living among us. You gave up your glory and every claim to deity to become sin. Brand this in my heart. Change me so I will reflect you to people around me.

Chapter 15

More Joy

Calvary, the Tomb, and Resurrection

Song 4:6 "Until the day breaks and the shadows flee, I will go to the mountain of myrrh and to the hill of incense."

It is the night of Calvary. The description of the bride that follows is what He viewed as Calvary unfolded. *"Shadows flee"* may refer to the shadows of the Old Testament no longer having center stage. In fact, when the reality came, the shadow was no longer needed except to confirm the real, or to help us appreciate the real. Now He is center stage.

For the shadows to flee, He had to go to the mountain of myrrh (the tomb) and the hill of incense (Calvary). It was on Calvary that He offered himself up as *"a fragrant offering and sacrifice to God." (Ephesians 5:1.)* The spices represent both His attributes and prayer. The hill of incense is the place of the ultimate incense offering, His life. Now the need for the altar of incense in the temple has ended, for He lives forever, making intercession for us. Indeed, the real has come.

"Until the day breaks" speaks of the resurrection. He had to endure darkness and death to enter the dawning day of resurrection. As He died, He saw her as the one with whom He was soon to experience intimate fellowship. This made the hill of Calvary and the tomb worth it.

Without Defect

Song 4:7 *"All beautiful you are my darling, there is no flaw in you."*

As He sees her through His sacrifice, He finds her perfect on this His wedding day. Her beauty comes from Him and His ransom price. Her beauty is the beauty of one washed by His blood. That He sees us with no flaw is amazing. When He washes us in His blood, we receive His righteousness. This righteousness is by faith alone. It is given to a company of people who love Him. No one person will ever be perfect on this earth except through His blood. Corporately what one member lacks another member has. Righteousness is imputed to us because of His blood. The glory we reflect individually will depend on how much time we spend in His presence and how much we seek Him. What He saw was the blood bought bride made perfect through His suffering. And He saw that company as they sought to know Him, being transformed by His glory.

Becoming

Song 4:8 *"Come with me from Lebanon my bride, come with me from Lebanon. Descend from the crest of Amana, from the top of Senir, the summit of Hermon, from the lions' dens and the mountain haunts of the leopards."*

Lebanon refers to the border-mountains that have separated Israel from the rest of the world. The bride is called from vacillating between the world and the Lord. Further, if she is to move on into the fullness of relationship with Him, she must forsake indecision.

Senir is the Amorite name for Mount Hermon and means a peak. [xvii] Amana means a fixed point or literally "a covenant".[xviii] The bride is in the border-mountains, the covenant. But this relationship includes more than the marriage contract, which she assented to at the banquet of wine. Besides this, it is time for her to enter deeper relationship with Him.

This is difficult. Her past has less hold on her than ever, but its hold is not completely broken. Following Him has a high price. The world says the price is too high. The question is not of turning her back on Him, rather, mixing the world with Him to make her life more comfortable. Coming with Him is to surrender control. She leaves behind humanistic methods to make life work. The wedding and the intimate relationship He offers signify a severing between her and the world. He calls. She must decide.

She is to come from the lower areas of these mountains too, from the lion's dens and the leopard haunts. Lions are ferocious and the leopards wily. Both are predators feeding on the weaker. The bride is being called from the place where brethren with problems prey upon one another. The leopard is a type of Antichrist, *Revelation 13:2.* She must forsake the false and everything that mimics the Lord. He calls her to forsake the shadow, the sham, and the counterfeit and embrace the real.

This is the first time He addresses her as bride. Until now, she was His darling. Now the work of Calvary is being finished in her behalf and He calls her His bride. No longer just betrothed, she is becoming His wife. The wedding is even now taking place. When He asks her to come from the border-mountains, He is calling her to forsake all others and cleave to Him.

For every believer, the wedding took place on Calvary, but we must appropriate it. The fullness of this will not happen until He comes, but we experience the reality of it now. This is not something for heaven. We must receive his many blessings and gifts. In fact, they are available to everyone, but many never receive them because they do not believe they are for them. This is true of entering an intimate relationship with Him. We must believe in the possibility and hear Him when He calls from the border-mountains. Most of us realize this after a long history with God.

Knowing Him as Bridegroom is a process. It is after much breaking, death, resurrection, and growth in Him. It is after much seeking. Frightened of what it means yet continuing to desire Him more, she views the cross in a new way. She sees His call to her considering His cross, His passion. Then He invites her into fellowship with Him in a way she never dreamed was possible.

The Enraptured Bridegroom as He Died

Song 4:9 "You have stolen my heart, my sister my bride; you have stolen my heart with one glance of your eyes, with one jewel of your necklace."

Stolen means to carry off by force. The believer willing to know Him carries off His heart by force. That is a statement worth thought. It is a further insight into His love for us, so we might love Him more.

One glance from her dove's eyes and one jewel from her necklace is enough to steal His heart, so great is His yearning for His bride. In *Song 1:10* she wore a necklace which was likely given by the King. In *Ezekiel 16:11* the Lord gave His beloved a necklace. The book of Esther shows Esther, who took with her only what the king's servant suggested when she went into the King. The king's servant is a type of the Holy Spirit preparing us for our King. His bride takes only that which the Holy Spirit suggests for her ornaments.

If left to us, we put on pseudo-humility, but the Holy Spirit clothes in genuine humility. We could put on a garment that says server of God across the chest. On the reverse side, it says server of self. The Holy Spirit clothes us in His righteousness, so we may go in unto the King. The Lord will destroy the garments and adornments of false humility. He will clothe us with humility.

Christ redeems us, and His blood makes us righteous. The Bridegroom clothes us in bridal garments and declares us beautiful. However, our part is to die to our own will to receive

Him. Calvary is the clearest picture of His love meant to draw us to Him.

Song 4:10 "How delightful is your love, my sister, my bride! How much more pleasing is your love than wine and the fragrance of your perfume than any spice."

Here we see the Bridegroom exulting in the bride's love. It is to Him more pleasing than wine. When the Bride uttered this phrase, she desired the kisses of His mouth, His reconciliation. This was the proof of her love. When the Bridegroom speaks these words, He proves it by dying. He wanted no blessing but her as His bride and gave His life to have her.

The fragrance she wears is not just a spice, but perfume in this passage is literally oils (NASB). The bride wears the anointing of the Lamb. This is the temple's anointing oil. The anointing oil consecrated that which (Ex. 40:9, Ex. 30) it touched. The anointing sets apart the one who carries it. This person is set apart first unto the Lord, then unto the ministry. If they are not set apart unto the Lord, then ministry will not be from God's heart.

Song 4:11 "Your lips drop sweetness as the honeycomb, my bride; milk and honey are under your tongue. The fragrance of your garments is like that of Lebanon."

The bride's speech is sweet. Bitterness does not come from her mouth. In contrast, consider James 3:9 *"With the tongue we praise our Lord and Father, and with it we curse men, who have been made in God's likeness. Out of the same mouth come praise and cursing..."*

When the bride enters that place of communion with the Bridegroom, she does not have harsh words for her brethren. When she prays, she does not condemn. Indeed, she seeks to speak words to others and in prayer that will help and heal.

The fragrance of Lebanon is the cedar (1Ki. 5:6). Her garments are moth proof. No worm can eat them to spoil them. These are her wedding garments given by the King, her robes of righteousness.

His Garden

Song 4:12 "You are a garden locked up, my sister, my bride. You are a spring enclosed, a sealed fountain. Your plants are an orchard of pomegranates with choice fruits, with henna and nard, nard and saffron, calamus and cinnamon, with every kind of incense tree, with myrrh and aloes and all the finest spices."

Picture this. The bride is a walled garden filled with marvelous fruitfulness. She is full of spices that are His attributes. How do we humans normally handle such abundance? If we think in terms of a garden once we have what we need, we want to give away the abundance to help others. This can be selfless giving, or an attempt to look good to others. If we think in terms of relationships, it gets interesting. Many believers appear to have the attributes of Christ and display how wonderful they are. In fact, they let all around them see their "Christ likeness" by using what is in their garden. The words they use pass muster but, underneath, is selfish-ambition and pride. They are using the spices of God (Christ's death) to get approval of others.

There is another choice. We can be a garden locked up, a spring enclosed, and a sealed fountain. What good is a locked garden? Who will enjoy the fruit? Who drinks from a sealed fountain? How do we give spiritual food and drink to others? The answers to these questions lay in the next several verses.

First note: His description of her as a garden locked. This means she is a virgin. This former man worshipper, playing the harlot with idols of the mind, is a virgin. She is locked up unto Him. Everything is for Him. Others may receive benefit from her life in other ways, but all within her garden is His.

In her garden is an orchard of pomegranates. The pomegranate was on the bottom of the High Priest's robe, alternating with bells. The bells tinkled when the High Priest walked *(Ex. 28:33)*. The pomegranate decorated the columns in Solomon's temple *(1Ki. 7)*. Its use on the High Priest's robe and its red and white flesh confirms the meaning to be righteousness through the blood of the Lamb.

Her Spices

Note the spices in her garden. These spices are in the anointing oil and the incense used in the temple. These are types and shadows of His death. Each of these spices comes forth with significant cost. They used myrrh for embalming. It was a product carried on the caravan that carried Joseph into slavery *(Genesis 38:25-27)*. Myrrh was one gift given to Joseph on the second trip his brothers made. It is interesting that myrrh played a prominent role in the life of a slave become leader. It plays a prominent role in the lives of slaves who become leaders today, too. A true anointing is birthed out of death. Esther used myrrh for 6 months to prepare her to go into the king *(Esther 2:12)*. The Wise-men gave Jesus myrrh at His birth *(Matt. 2:12)*. On the cross the soldiers gave it to Jesus to drink *(Mk. 14:23)*. The disciples used myrrh to embalm Him *(John. 19:39)*. To be a bride prepared for her Bridegroom, we must allow the myrrh to do its work.

Frankincense is one of the incense trees. We scored the tree to make the incense. [xix] The tree is wounded. Only as wounding takes place can she appropriate this attribute. This spice fixes the odor. This is a lasting anointing. It does a deep work. Counterfeit anointing's are fun while they happen, but when the "anointed one" leaves, no real growth has taken place. They smell good for a short time because the one ministering avoided suffering. In fact, true anointing's work in lives until we are in the presence of the King eternally.

Another spice, calamus, is a fragrant reed and literally means erect. [xx] In Revelation 11, calamus is the rod that measures of the court of the temple for judgment. In the book of Ezekiel calamus measures the new temple. This reed measures us against the measure of God. We often measure ourselves against each other and believe we are better than our neighbor. However, when we are measured against the Lord, we fall short.

Henna or camphire is a shrub with white flowers. They used its leaves and flowers when dried and crushed as a dye for hair and beard.[xxi] Even the fruitfulness of our lives needs to be crushed, so we love Him.

Nard is the spikenard we read about earlier.[xxii] This is a very expensive fragrance and used to anoint the Lord's feet before his death and burial. This ointment is rose-red and costly.

Saffron is the autumn crocus highly valued for aroma and flavor and a vivid yellow dye.[xxiii]

Aloes was a tree about the size of the olive and had an aromatic resin. This tree had to be wounded to give forth the fragrance.[xxiv]

To harvest cinnamon, the inner bark of the tree is stripped and dried. We must cut the branches when they are about an inch thick. Similarly, often the believer feels as if their branches were pruned. Pruning is painful. Pain brings the attributes of God. These spices are types of His suffering, and His holiness.

These sound great. If you have these in your life, then you are right with God. If only this statement were true. Much in religious life resembles these spices. Many people appear to be humble, broken servants. So how can we know?

We must remember, God may show us what is happening, so we will not be ensnared. However, the person putting on the religious show has not seen the truth yet. They may never see it, or they are in the process that will reveal the truth to them. Our responsibility is to discern and avoid doing likewise. Beyond that we are to pray. We are not called to broadcast to the world the names of those we suspect since we could see things incorrectly. If we will pray, then perhaps that misguided person will see soon. But there are signs we can look for.

The Adulteress

The adulterous wife uses these spices. In *Proverbs 7:17* the adulterous wife says, *"I have perfumed by bed with myrrh, aloes, and cinnamon."* Verse *21* tells us, *"With persuasive words, she led him astray, she seduced him with her smooth talk."* She told him she was dead to self. After all, the spices prove she suffered. She said God spoke to her, and He anointed her. She told him what he wanted to hear, and he fell for it because he wanted to indulge the flesh. One in this position is seduced into a counterfeit of the relationship between the Bridegroom and the bride. The adulterous wife leads the unwary to her "anointed" bed using scripture to deceive.

Who is this adulterous wife then? It is the person who is worshipping other gods the way Israel worshipped other gods along with the Lord. The adulterous wife worships her own will and way. Her gods are power, notoriety, control, and a host of others, large and small. She knows how to use the things of God to look holy. This person knows the word and can use it to fool many.

It is interesting to note that on her bed she uses myrrh, aloes, and cinnamon. In *Psalm 45:8* at the wedding it is said of the Lord that: *"All thy garments smell of myrrh, aloes, and cassia."* The adulterous wife has myrrh, aloes, and cinnamon on her bed. The bed shows us it means seduction. Cinnamon and cassia are similar in smell. Indeed, myrrh and aloes embalmed Jesus and were part of the anointing oil. The adulterous wife uses spiritual gifts and attributes of God to seduce. We must pray and live in the word, so we can tell the difference between the real and the false. A sign of the real is that you are led into a deeper relationship with Him. You die to your own will and become alive to His will.

Scripture shows another woman that uses the spices. She is the harlot. In *Revelation 13:18, the harlot trades in "cargoes of cinnamon and spice, of incense, myrrh and frankincense, of wine and olive oil."* Before, we saw how the adulterous wife put the spices on her bed to seduce. Here, the harlot merchandises the anointing. They used the anointing for profit. This is sad since anointing's for ministry bless God's people. This person probably had a true anointing. They may even move in a true anointing now, but often they also move in a counterfeit anointing. In time if not solved, it can become only counterfeit, just fleshly ministry. The purpose of the ministry is to gain fame or fortune.

The harlot trades in "cargoes...and bodies and souls of men." Revelation 18:11-12 Bodies are numbers to make the work look successful. The more bodies present, the greater the king looks. Kings do not view people as God's precious sheep to be tended with tender care. They are only cogs in the gears of the king's power. They are merchandise, a commodity to use and throw away when no longer useful or will no longer submit to autocratic rule.

The harlot uses the word of the Lord to get her way. She comes saying, "I have heard from God," and she buys the hearts of people hungry for spiritual reality. Elsewhere in scripture, people with this problem are called false prophets. They once carried a true word from God, but now they have prostituted it for the praise of men or the riches of this earth. Is there hope for this person? There is always hope. Judging them and spreading gossip about them will not set them free, although prayer may. If you think you know someone like this, think again. Our judgment is very faulty. This is not written so we can judge one another. It is written so we can know the symptoms and avoid the causes of this problem in our own lives.

The Pure Bride

The bride has these spices as well. They are not on her bed to seduce the unwary. She does not merchandise them. She is not a collector of admirers trading in men's bodies and souls. The bride is full of Him and His attributes. In fact, her garden is locked for Him. The anointing is the overflow of her life in Him. If she uses the anointing, she will end up an adulterous wife. If she stays locked up unto Him, she faces no danger of that.

The bride decided along the way to give up slavery. She did not realize it, but that meant she yielded the enslaving passions that could make her use the things of God. We are not just slaves to people. We are slaves of the enemy of our souls when we believe his lies and live, considering them. This entire way of life she forsook, even though it was where she placed her trust. She suffered turmoil, confusion, and pain, but that decision is the reason she is a garden locked up today. Further, she decided for this day by day for years. This is not a onetime decision. Every day, she had to refuse deception and choose until truth became a way of life.

So, the question is, if she is locked up unto Him, how can others receive from her life? *Genesis 49:22 "Joseph is a fruitful vine, a fruitful vine near a spring, whose branches hang over a wall."* If my apple tree hangs over in my neighbor's yard, they have a legal right to the apples on that part of the tree. But And for the bride's garden others can only have the abundance of her garden as it spills out over the garden wall. Everything else belongs to the Bridegroom. This is the abundant fruitfulness of intimate relationship with Him.

She is a Fountain

Song *4:15 "You are a garden fountain, a well of flowing water streaming down from Lebanon."*

The Bride is a locked fountain and a well of streaming water. Notice that the fruitful vine of Joseph grows near a spring. Whatever flows out under the garden gate is the overflow. Whatever hangs over the wall is the extra for others. The bride only opens for her Beloved. Because of this, God's gifts are not prostituted. She never uses His gifts and incense to draw others to herself. The bride will not boast of her Christlikeness. Her life does not avoid suffering, for to avoid suffering is to avoid true Christlikeness. She wants to know Him and become like Him. Since suffering is a part of that, so be it.

The bride is a well of flowing water, a spring. *John 4:14b "Indeed the water I give him will become in him a spring of water welling up to eternal life."* The Lord is the source of this living water.

Until He Comes

Virgin garden untouched by man,
mystery of God's mighty plan.
Locked and sealed, the gates are barred,
until He comes with nail prints scarred.

The gates fly open at His touch,
no other hand can do this much.
The garden waits on Him alone,
until He comes to love His own.

For Reflection

1.   What stands between you and the knowledge you are dearly loved? Ask Him what scriptures you need to stand in to change your thinking.

2.   What must you be set free from to be a locked garden and an enclosed fountain?

3.   How can you cooperate with the death He knows you need to die? If you do not know, ask Him.

4.   Is the sin of your past keeping you from being able to receive from Him that you are a virgin garden? Write down what He wants to tell you about this.

5.   Will you commit to Him and allow Him to be everything to you, no matter the cost?

6.   Will you give up your desire for acceptance and love by others and receive from Him not only relationship with Him, but with the others He chooses for you?

Prayer

Lord, help me see your great love for me. Help me view your death as you mean it to be viewed.

Set me free from the tendencies in my life to desire the approval and love of others, so I may be completely yours. Show me what keeps me from intimacy with you. I repent of my harlot tendencies. Help me be willing for the stripping and crushing that is needed to bring me into intimacy with you. I need to see you. I need to keep my eyes off the distractions, but I cannot do this on my own.

Help me embrace the myrrh needed in my life instead of finding ways out of your pruning and correction. Help me turn to you day by day, so I will find everything I need to walk in intimacy with you. Strengthen me with your presence. As I seek, you let me find you so that you will fill my heart.

Recreate me into your virgin garden, your well of flowing water. Purify my heart and my mind until all I want is you. Then let the abundance of relationship with you hang out over the garden wall to cause others to love you.

Chapter 16

Consummation

Heart to Heart

This next portion of scripture is possible only for the resurrected bride. As she sees His sacrifice in the earlier passages, she responds to His invitation to come with Him if she did not already do so. Further, she commits to whatever it takes to bring her into an intimate relationship with Him. No price is too high to pay for that intimacy.

Song 4:16 "Awake, north wind, and come, south wind! Blow on my garden that its fragrance may spread abroad. Let my lover come into his garden and taste its choice fruits."

The winds, especially the north winds, bring the freeze of winter. North winds are often a type of trials. The bride desires the north winds of adversity and the winds of spring, the south winds of fruitfulness to blow upon her life. This blows fragrance from her garden to the Bridegroom. That is the purpose of these spices in her garden, to delight the Bridegroom. It takes trial to bring forth the fragrance of each spice. The south winds warmth is necessary to the growth of the bride. It takes all the seasons to bring forth fruitfulness.

I Corinthians 10:16 "Is not the cup of thanksgiving for which we give thanks a participation in the blood of Christ? And is not the bread that we break a participation in the body of Christ?

The word participation ˣˣᵛ in this passage is "koinonia", (Greek) and means partnership, participation, communion, or fellowship. There is fellowship with Him when we share in His sufferings. The word communion ˣˣᵛⁱ means mutual participation or intimate fellowship. Communion takes place in the garden. That is consummation. When we receive communion at church, that is a visible symbol of what should happen in the believer's life.

Communion or consummation is intricately entwined with His suffering as evidenced by the elements of communion, His body and blood. His cross must be central for the close communion of the Song of Songs to take place. In fact, the fellowship we enjoy with Him includes the fellowship of sharing in His sufferings. True communion or communication happens in the context of that fellowship. Real communion does not exist without this. We are only fulfilling empty rituals and are frauds trying hard to look real. We will not know the reality of the locked garden with His presence. Apart from this, He exists for us as the God who stands at a distance. Yet, we are the ones who hold Him off by our refusal to embrace difficulty to have Him.

We want to separate suffering from the process. Difficulty is not pleasant. We try to avoid suffering all along the way until we realize that suffering will purify us. Our false ideals and beliefs are important to us. It will be painful to lose them. Suffering is giving up that which we are attached to, though the things we are attached to are useless or false. When these false ideas fill our minds and hearts, He cannot. That is why we must fellowship, by sharing in His sufferings. Then these things die, and we make room for Him.

We are called to die daily to our own will. That is suffering until we come to know Him intimately. Then this death becomes closeness of fellowship. Now we understand His death and the love that embraced that death. His will becomes ours because of love.

He Gathers Her Suffering

Song 5:1 "I have come into my garden, my sister, my bride. I have gathered my myrrh with my spice. I have eaten my honeycomb with my honey; I have drunk my wine and my milk."

When He enters His garden, the first thing He does is gather myrrh and spices. That is death and suffering. He gathers His sufferings in her life. This is part of the fellowship, along with the honey, wine, and milk are the spices, and the myrrh.

Next, He eats the honey and drinks the milk and wine. Honey is sweet. In her garden, He finds sweetness. God promised the Israelites a land flowing with milk and honey. Wine is a type of blessing and abundance. The Lord has come into His garden and found abundant fruitfulness.

The Israelite's disobedience in the desert kept them from entering the land with milk and honey. Their descendants entered. Years later, because of disobedience, the Israelites were taken captive to Babylon and Assyria. They lost the abundance through unbelief and disobedience. Unlike the Israelites, the bride learns to trust and obey. She is a garden full of the blessing of God. **She** is the land that was promised, flowing with milk and honey.

Song 5:1b "Eat, O friends, and drink; drink your fill, O lovers."

The garden has abundance for anyone who comes, but others cannot partake of it unless He is in it. Only when the bride walks in intimacy with Him, should she share what is in her garden with others. Fellowship with Him in His sufferings keeps her humble. Closeness with Him will naturally bring fruitfulness for others. As He partakes first, the overflow grows over the garden wall and goes out to the world. Others can only have the overflow.

For Reflection

1. What behaviors do you use to avoid suffering? Do you run from Him? How about staying over busy? Do you avoid relationships? Perhaps you practice a more hermit like life?

2. What behaviors and attitudes separate you from receiving the intimate fellowship with the Bridegroom as you go through difficulty? Do you struggle with anger, bitterness, or a sense of entitlement that you deserved better?

3. Look back on your life. How has your avoidance kept you from knowing Him?

4. Tell Him what you have been doing and yield it to Him.

5. What step can you take today to draw closer to Him, even in difficulty?

Prayer

Lord, I held you at arms-length so many times, run from you, let other things steal my time and avoided things you have wanted me to embrace. Forgive me for wanting comfort more than I wanted your presence. Help me love you and want you more. Help me die to the self-life that rises within me and defines my life.

Take my broken heart and mold it into a heart that loves you alone. Show me what it means to have no other lovers. Show me how to fix my eyes on you and show me the next step in my journey into intimacy with you. Help me keep even good things such as ministry, family or work from replacing the best thing, heart to heart fellowship with you.

Chapter 17

Asleep Again

The Koinonia of Suffering

A minor change occurs in the last half of Song of Songs. Though the entire book is written to the individual and the corporate bride, the first four chapters apply more readily to the individual. The last four have a higher incidence of application to the corporate bride. This is as it should be. The dealings that bring the bride to the point of intimacy are personal. The dealings after revealing true communion are to bring her not only into closer relationship with her Lord, but with His people. In fact, only through true union with Him is unity among believers is possible. Unity sought in any other way brings conformity, legalism, or syncretism. In other words, we call it unity, but it is not the unity of the Spirit of God, but a man made and false unity. This type of unity will end in compromise that leads to idolatry.

God's Unity

Before the spiritual consummation, the bride lived out of an old dynamic. That old dynamic kept her from having a genuine relationship with others. Now she lives considering His truth. Before, she hurt others because of the lack of wholeness in her life. Now she can love and accept others because of the transformation inside of her. She offers love based on the unity that the Father, Son and Holy Spirit enjoy.

John 17:21 "that all of them may be one, Father, just as you are in me and I am in you. May they also be in us so that the world may believe that you have sent me." Also, see the rest of John 17.

The efforts of man cannot manufacture this unity. It is God produced through the intimate fellowship of His bride with Him. Remember, everything of value we possess is the overflow of communion with Him. In fact, if we have the fruit of unity with Him, hanging over the wall, then others will pick the fruit. If others have the fruit of unity hanging over their wall, then we will be able to pick their fruit. This is God's method to produce unity. The unity that exists in heaven does not have idolatry mixed with it. *Matt. 6:10 "your kingdom come, your will be done on earth as it is in heaven."*

If we allow our will to become His, we will know unity with Him and others. Or to put it another way, if we know intimacy with Him, our will, shall become His will and we will know unity with other believers that join Him in the secret place.

The Complacent Bride

Song 5:2 "I slept but my heart was awake. Listen, my lover is knocking: Open to me my sister, my darling, my dove, my flawless one. My head is drenched with dew, my hair with dampness of the night."

The word slept in this passage comes from the root word. That means to be languid, lax, and weary. [xxvii] His bride slept because of complacency, but her heart was awake to love. The word wake in this passage means to open the eyes.[xxviii] Though the eyes of her heart were awake, she chose to sleep. It was while the farmer slept that the enemy sowed tares among the wheat. *(Matthew 13:25)*

When the Lord prayed on Gethsemane, the disciples slept rather than pray. *(Matthew 26:36-46)* If the farmer had not slept, the tares could not have been sown among the wheat. If the disciples prayed, they would have been prepared for the Lord's death more fully. Jesus told Peter to watch and pray so he would not fall into temptation. *(Mark 14:38)*

When we bow to complacency rather than bending our knees to pray, we are easily tempted because we do not know the heart of God. In prayer, we not only lay our petitions before the Lord, but we also hear from Him what is on His heart. That hearing keeps us straight with Him. When the enemy comes, we cannot be tempted because the Lord has spoken to us in our prayer time. This strengthens us in the areas the enemy attacks. Calvary's confusion would have been diminished had the disciples prayed while the Lord was at Gethsemane.

When we are asleep, the Lord comes to rouse us to fellowship with him. Complacency robs us of the ability to respond to His call. The bride has become complacent because everything is so wonderful now that she has this new closeness with the Lord. Genuine joy is hers. Life has never been so good. It is easy to take Him for granted. So, He comes to her, his head covered with dew of the night. This is the dew of Gethsemane before His death. He wants her to understand that complacency is not her place. Prayer is. He is the intercessor lamb.

There is another picture. In this passage the word for hair [xxix] means hair that is cut short, and the word head means head of the family or clan. [xxx] The bride's long hair is a sign of subjection. Short hair is a sign of authority for the Bridegroom. The dew of intercession is upon the head of authority. He is not only the one who prayed at Gethsemane and died on Calvary, but also rose to make intercession for His bride. He is the King, the Holy One.

Though complacency is a natural occurrence to one who has suffered and now knows peace, she must not stay there.

Song 5:3 "I have taken off my robe. Must I put it on again? I have washed my feet, must I soil them again?"

This is a curious reply from one who has known the intimacy of communion. This is not strange from someone who is complacent, however. She has taken off her robe of righteousness to rest. This does not mean she is sinning, but it means she is not ready to meet the challenges of the day. Facing life without the robe He gives her is to invite failure.

She washed her feet. The feet contact the world. They are our means of walking. She does not want to walk and get them dirty. Indeed, without her robe, she cannot walk before men at all. She would rather stay in her place of complacent slumber, so she does not have to face the challenges.

There is hope in the heart of every believer that we can grow without trials. We want every circumstance to be comfortable and convenient. We are of the tribe of Issachar wanting the pleasant land. *(Gen. 49:15-16)* Coming into an intimate relationship with Him does not kill that hope. It can take a lifetime for that desire to die. We died to our ideals and expectations. In their place, we now have Him. His love has healed our hearts in a way that words won't describe. However, we still hope for comfort and convenience. We want to grow closer to Him without challenge. To go among people will bring complications anew. It is easier to lay aside the robe and wash our feet. Convenience temps us to lie complacently and refuse entry to the One who has made the wholeness possible. To receive Him is to receive the people He died to purchase.

Song 5:4 My lover thrust his hand through the latch opening. My heart began to pound for him."

The Nail Pierced Hand

It is not until He puts His hand through the hole in the door and she sees His nail pierced hand that she responds with love. His hand reminds her of His love for her and His love for all men. A glimpse of His nail-scarred hand brings the complacent to their feet. When Thomas saw those hands, He cried out, "My Lord and my God." (John 20:27-28) The Lord's sacrifice is central to the bride's response. From the beginning to the end of His song the cross will be central. He is ever revealing Himself to the bride as the Lamb. It is that revelation alone with the power to challenge her out of sin and complacency when she yields to them. We do a disservice to one another when our preaching and worship center on man. If we center it upon the Lamb, the people of God will grow like never before.

Song 5:5 "I arose to open for my lover, and my hands dripped with myrrh, my fingers with flowing myrrh on the handles of the lock."

First, notice the lock. The door mentioned had a latch that was from either side. The person outside reached in an opening and opened the latch unless it was locked. Not only was the bride complacent, but that complacency locked Him out of close communion with her. Even His nail-scarred hand could not open the latch she had locked. She had to grant Him entrance.

Her fingers and hands dripped with myrrh. Out of this place of complacency, comes repentance as she dies to the comfort she desires. Myrrh drips from a newly scored tree and her heart is that tree. The myrrh flows upon the lock. Whatever is in her life that represents the lock must receive the myrrh. In fact, death must cover everything that holds her back from the Lord and His people.

There is another meaning inherent in the flowing myrrh since, it is a major ingredient of the anointing oil. His death anoints her in a new way to minister. The bride may be in a complacent place, but love draws her out of it and sends her forth with a new anointing for ministry. It is a ministry that shows forth the death of the Bridegroom. This ministry is the most needed ministry in the church and world. Our advertising about our wonderful miracles and signs will not draw people to love God, but a true glimpse of His suffering will.

We do not need more public relations firms to help us build big ministries that focus on man. We need nobodies that know God to show forth His death in their lives. That alone will draw men to Him. Jesus' death should not become an advertising gimmick. The anointing the bride carries shows forth His death not as a gimmick, but as a way of life.

Trained by Absence

Song 5:6 "I opened for my lover, but my lover had left; He was gone. My heart sank at his departure. I looked for him but did not find him. I called him but he did not answer."

When the bride opened, He was gone. The purpose of this is to cause the bride to desire Him again. He wants her to follow. Thus, His absence is a key to the bride learning to yearn for His presence constantly. His provision for her as her husband includes His constant presence, but she must not become complacent, or He will need to be absent to train her.

She looked for Him outside the door. She looked for Him in the last place His presence was. It is a new day, and we must search for His presence today. She called to Him in prayer, and He did not answer. *Song 5:7 "The watchmen found me as they made their rounds in the city. They beat me, they bruised me; they took away my cloak, those watchmen of the walls."*

It is dangerous to lie in complacency and suffer His absence because of that complacency. There are those who have seen the intimacy of relationship between the bride and her lover. They are jealous of that relationship but unwilling to pay the price to have it. These people are often in leadership. They may be in the position of the watchmen of Israel.

If the bride suffers a lack of His presence, these watchmen will find her and abuse her as her slave holders once did. They will take advantage of His absence to show her they are better than her.

The word cloak in NIV is literally veil. It comes from the root word that means to conquer, overlay, or spread. The queen, as a symbol of subjection, is veiled. It keeps her beauty alone for Him. No one else can see her beauty unless He desires to show it. To take away her veil was to uncover her beauty before all curious eyes. Thus, it was a symbol of her special standing in the eyes of the King to be veiled. The jealous watchmen took it away to shame her.

None of this would have happened if she had not been asleep in complacency, if she had not desired comfort. He meant her to intercede and watch with Him, but she was not ready. Because she was not ready in prayer, she fell prey to the watchmen. Had she been praying and in His presence, the watchmen couldn't have shamed her.

This feels so much like the past that for a moment, she feels marriage intimacy was a dream. Despair takes over as the enemy whispers she will always be beaten. In her heart, however, she knows better. If fear comes, it will not receive a long audience. She has learned the lessons well and knows the difference between the enemy's lies and God's truths.

Awaken Me

You come to awaken me.
I hear you with my heart.
But Lord, my heart chooses
to lie at rest for a little longer.
So hard, so hard, this call has been.
So long I have fought to find you.
Can I not rest?
Can I not sit out a few battles?
Will I ever know normal?

Your intercession, your sacrifice
Is upon your Kingship
You come to one who does not deserve,
who cannot yet see the fullness
of the mystery.

Locked out,
you leave to draw me on,

to make me
hungry and thirsty for you

No one helps me.
Then I realize no one can.
My heart must find you.
My heart must learn to hold you.
My heart must learn that
Rest is found in no other.
Love is found in no other.

Your will cannot be understood
apart from your presence
My mind, so mixed between love
and the world's offers
can only find resolution in you.

Awaken my heart yet again.
Awaken my heart to You.

For Reflection

1. What series of events causes you to choose complacency?

2. Do you jump up when He comes to the door, or do you hesitate?

3. In what way, did you find the watchmen could not help you?

4. How can you avoid complacency in the future?

5. What strongholds in the culture woo you into complacency?

6. What scriptures can you memorize to help you overcome the tendency to choose complacency?

7. Can you admit to others that you failed and need Him? Ask the Lord to bring others you can share this with this week.

Prayer

Lord, you have all authority and power. You are the head, the King. You are glorious in your intercession on behalf of man. How can One who is above all become sin for us mortals? How can you desire us? Yet you gladly chose both. Help me understand how blessed I am to have you pursuing me. Help me love you, as you deserve to be loved.

Do the work in me that will set me free from complacency. Teach me how to seek you and find you by searching for you with all my heart. Show me the way to find my rest in you rather than complacency. Transform me so my will becomes your will. May your beauty be what others will see when they look at my life.

Chapter 18

The Bridegroom

Sharing the Bridegroom

Now we notice the beginning of true ministry for the bride. Ministry comes after complacency that causes His absence. How? Real ministry comes when we least expect it.

During the years we strived to be someone that God's people will look up to and revere, little real flowed through our lives. It took slavery, death, and the tomb to make us real. The death of ambition, pride, self-centeredness, and idealism was necessary, so we become real. When real ministry comes, we no longer crave it because our desires for the praise of men are refined. In fact, to minister can be frightening. What if others hurt us again? We sometimes feel it is easier to stay in complacency and safety. There is one problem; the Lord is not in that safe place. It is our seeking for Him as we come out of the safe, complacent place that leads us back into ministry, much to our surprise.

Song 5:9 "How is your beloved better than others, most beautiful of women? How is your beloved better than others, that you charge us so?"

Having been in complacency and stirred out of it by the Lord's absence, the Bride has gone on a search for Him. Unashamed to let others know she is lacking His presence; she becomes vulnerable in the same way she was during hard days before the blessings made her complacent. Her devotion to Him stirs the hearts of the friends, so they ask how He is better than others. When they see this devotion, they need to know He is worth giving up their ideals, ambitions, pride and self-centeredness. They need to know if the pain of losing everything as she did is worth it. Her search for Him provokes the question. Her answer is the beginning of real ministry. The answer points to the cross. Describing Him shows Him in His death, and His kingship. The bride does not give a talk on Ten Points to a Holy Life. She does not come up with a new teaching to win their loyalty. She shares with them that which has made her free, seeing Him. If she helps them understand what she sees, then they can pay the price as she did. They will receive the intimacy she knows and delight the Bridegroom's heart.

Even as we were, the joy set before Him that enabled Him to suffer. He is the joy set before us. We can suffer the loss of ideals and lies we live by because the Lamb is before us. Because of what she learned; the bride tells the questioners He is that joy. She sets Him before them.

Many today say we must count the cost, but counting the cost does not mean to dwell on it. The way the bride paid the price was by seeing Him, not by being reminded of the high cost. Our focus must be on His cross, not ours. His church must emphasize the Lamb in the midst of the throne. He paid the ultimate price. When we know Him, we understand His price and are enabled to say yes to wherever His will takes us.

Song 5:10 "My lover is radiant and ruddy, outstanding among ten thousand."

Ruddy speaks of His blood and radiance, His purity. He is set apart from the rest by purity and the blood of His sacrifice. The word radiant means dazzling. He is dazzling in His purity. He is the Spotless Lamb. Hebrews 1:3 "The son is the radiance of God's glory and the exact representation of His being." When we see the Bridegroom, we see the glory and being of God.

Matthew 17:1-8 "After six days Jesus took with him Peter, James and John the brother of James, and led them up a high mountain by themselves. There he was transfigured before them. His face shone like the sun, and his clothes became as white as the light. Just then, there appeared before them Moses and Elijah, talking with Jesus.

Peter said to Jesus, "Lord, it is good for us to be here. If you wish, I will put up three shelters-one for you, one for Moses and one for Elijah."

While he was still speaking, a bright cloud enveloped them, and a voice from the cloud said, "This is my Son, whom I love; with him I am well pleased. Listen to Him!"

When the disciples heard this, they fell facedown to the ground, terrified. But Jesus came and touched them. "Get up," He said, "Don't be afraid." When they looked up, they saw no one except Jesus."

Peter wanted to build three shelters, or literally tabernacles. One tabernacle was for Moses (Law), another for Elijah (Prophets) and the third for Jesus. The Law and the Prophets found fulfillment in Jesus Christ. They are a type of the last move of God, the Old Covenant. Jesus is the guarantor of a New Covenant. We are not to build tabernacles, houses of worship, or monuments to the last move of God. In fact, we cannot move forward with the Lord when our eyes are looking back. The past kept the disciples from understanding who Jesus was. It is the same with us.

Astounding Works of God

Though I understood the truth of this passage as it pertained to the Church, I had not personalized it. One day during my prayer time, the Lord led me to this passage. Specifically verse three, *"Just then there appeared before them Moses and Elijah, talking with Jesus."* As I read this one verse, I heard the Lord speak in my heart. "Moses and Elijah are your past. Your past has been difficult. You cannot see what I desire to do in your life today, because you view everything through your past. You believe I will only give you a tiny blessing, like a small candle lit in the center of a large dark room. I want to do astounding things for you."

That day I learned even the move of God in my life to bring me to truth and wholeness (that move was like captivity in Babylon) could keep me from Him today. God was with me during the years of slavery and the captivity in Babylon. He was with me and with the Church when so many leaders beat the sheep. That past move of purging kept me from seeing what the Lord desired to do today, as surely as the excitements that I enjoyed in the church did. He wants to do something wonderful.

When we see the radiant Lord, we hear the voice out of the cloud telling us, "Listen to Him!" The response of the heart to the voice of the Father is holy fear. We fall on our faces, and like the disciples see, *"no one but Jesus."* We need to hear His voice today. The past move of God keeps us from seeing the Son in His glory.

I Peter 1:18-19 "For you know that it was not with perishable things such as silver or gold that you were redeemed from the empty way of life handed down to you from your forefathers, but with the precious blood of Christ, a lamb without blemish or defect."

He is described as ruddy in Song 5:10 because He shed His life for us. The past was an empty way of life. The behaviors we took part in as slaves were empty. We were redeemed with the precious blood of the Lamb. Why is it worthwhile to pay the price to be free? It is because He purchased us. The one who is the radiance of God's glory died to set us free from our past life. We are free from the futile ways of life handed down to us from our forefathers. The emphasis is not on our cost, but on His. It is in seeing the cost to Him we can say yes to our cost.

The number ten thousand stands for an uncountable number. Among the host of heaven and earth, He is the Lord, the Only One. There is no other who rules victoriously.

He is Trustworthy

Song 5:11 *"His head is purest gold, His hair is wavy, as black as a raven."*

The head of pure gold tells us there is no mixture in His headship. He is not like others who claimed to have authority over us but were using us. We can submit to His headship and be safe.

Ephesians 1:22 "And God placed all things under his feet and appointed him to be head over everything for the church." He is the only one who was given to be head over the church. He is totally trustworthy because of His sacrifice.

The wavy black hair means that His hair was short. That is a sign of authority, even as the bride's long black hair is a sign of subjection.

Jn. 10:17 "The reason my Father loves me is that I lay down my life — only to take it up again. No one takes it from me, but I lay it down of my own accord. I have authority to lay it down and authority to take it up again. This command I received from my Father."

Jesus had authority to raise the dead, heal the sick, preach the good news, die and be raised to life.

The black hair is a picture of His humanity as well. The gold head speaks of His divinity. If He were not human and divine, there would be no salvation, relationship, or chance for the end of slavery and a new life.

He Has Dove's Eyes and the Fulness of Deity

Song 5:12 *"His eyes are like doves, by the water streams, washed in milk, mounted like jewels."*

This next description is wonderful. The bride's eyes, like doves, are a must in view of the Lord's dealings with her. But the Bridegroom also has dove's eyes. This is amazing. He has eyes only for His bride, only for you.

Water is a type of the Holy Spirit. The Spirit led Him when He was here on earth. The Spirit was His teacher as He grew to become a man. Jesus was the Word of God that became flesh and lived among us. He spoke, and He formed the world. Yet, as man and God, He was led of the Spirit.

Water streams are channels of water with the emphasis on the channel. His channel was the will of the Father. He did as He saw the Father doing. Because of love, He saw and did only what the Father was doing. *John 5:19: "I tell you the truth, the Son can do nothing by himself; he can do only what he sees his Father doing, because whatever the Father does the Son also does."*

His eyes were washed in milk. These are the first principles of God's word, *(Heb. 5:12)*. To understand what the Father was doing, the elemental principles of the word bathed His eyes as He grew from a boy to a man. The one who was the Word of God had to be instructed because He gave up His glory to be born as a human. *Luke 2:52 "And Jesus grew in wisdom and stature, and in favor with God and men."*

We must understand these same elemental principles. The Holy Spirit gave Him understanding of His role in salvation. That is one of the elemental principles. He committed to whatever the Holy Spirit showed Him and therefore fulfilled the will of God. *(Jn. 17:4)*

The Bridegroom's eyes are mounted like jewels. This expression means to be set in fullness as a stone in a ring. [xxxi]

Colossians 1:19 "For God was pleased to have all his fullness dwell in Him."

The eyes that see do so because the fullness of God dwells in Him. This fullness is so full it cannot be measured. The bride speaks of a Lord that has all the fullness in Him. She has experienced this fullness in her own life. *Colossians 1:19b "And you have that fullness in Christ..."*

We often live as if this fullness is for someone else because of the lies of the enemy. The bride practices believing in what the scripture says about her until it becomes a part of her. His fullness belongs to His bride.

Song 5:13 "His cheeks are like beds of spice yielding perfume. His lips are like lilies dripping with myrrh."

The way spices yield perfume is through pain to the plant. His cheeks are beds of spices. The aroma is endless.

Isaiah 52:14 "... his appearance was so disfigured, beyond that of any man." The picture the bride describes is one who was so smitten and scarred that the spices will be never ending.

Even as His torment brought forth the aroma, it brought forth myrrh from His lips. He shared about His death many times with His disciples. He said that He spoke only as He heard from His Father. Because He spoke as He heard, He was crucified. Men despised and rejected Him because He spoke the truth. Further, He knew the truth will ensure His death and yet He was not silent.

Matthew 10:18-19 tells us we will be handed over to governors and kings. In that day, we are not to worry what we say, God will speak through us. We too will have lips anointed with myrrh. Only He knows the outcome. The myrrh anointed lips speak of submission to the Father, speaking as we hear. Myrrh means dying to our concerns as to the outcome of our obedience to Him. Therefore, dying instead of believing we have suffered enough.

Works, Authority and Sonship

Song 5:14 "His arms are rods of gold set with chrysolite. His body is polished ivory decorated with sapphires."

The word arm in this passage is hand and the word rods are rings.[xxxii] His hands look as if they are covered with gold rings set with golden stones. The hands often speak of the works. He made the world. His golden hands show forth His perfect works. *(Jn. 17:4)* The rings speak of His authority. The signet ring of the King carried His power and authority with its imprint. The prodigal son's father gave him a golden ring. A golden ring is a sign of Sonship. His hands show forth the glory of His works, the authority of His kingdom and His everlasting Sonship.

The body of ivory signifies His pure manhood. *Hebrews 10:5,10 "Sacrifice and offering you did not desire, but a body you prepared for me.... We have been made holy by the sacrifice of the body of Jesus Christ once for all."*

The father prepared Him a body, so it could be sacrificed that we, His body on the earth, could be holy. Because of our flawed humanity, we need Him to make us holy through His blood.

The sapphires speak of the heavens and His grace. This is a picture of His glorified body. He rules and reigns eternally in heaven because of His sacrifice and we, His body, bear His sufferings through grace that became ours when His body was broken for us.

The Glorified King Without Defect

Song 5:15 "His legs are pillars of marble set on bases of pure gold. His appearance is like Lebanon, choice as its cedars."

Marble goes through metamorphosis when limestone goes deep into the earth through geological activity. Heat, pressure and hot liquid solvents act upon the limestone. Grains of calcite change as well as minerals. The more intense the heat and pressure on these minerals, the finer the marble. The fine marble is white and most valuable. Ancient buildings of fine marble still stand today.

This is a picture of our Lord in the tomb. He entered the tomb the God-man; He exited the tomb the glorified King. The pressure of suffering in His life produced a change. He became the firstborn from the dead.

The pillar holds up the roof on a building. This is a picture of strength. The Lord walked with strength upon the earth. He did not vacillate or run in fear. In fact, He stood firm and declared what He heard from the Father.

His legs are set in bases of pure gold. His feet are pure divinity, even as His head is. From head to toe, He is perfect and both head and foot are gold in Song of Songs. Since we are to be like Him, this means our thoughts and our walk must be refined as gold is refined, so we reflect His glory and His holiness.

The word Lebanon means white [xxxiii] and the word appearance is countenance. [xxxiv] Lebanon is an exquisite mountainous country. When the bride looks at the Lord, she sees His purity and His beauty. His countenance is choice as its cedars. The cedars were used to build the temple, Solomon's house, and many other buildings. Cedar lasts because insects will not eat it. The cedar stands for sinless-ness, as does the word Lebanon. The wonder and the glory of the Christian life is His sinless perfection. In almost every description of Him she speaks of this.

Lover and Friend

Song *5:16 "His mouth is sweetness itself; he is altogether lovely. This is my lover, this is my friend, O daughters of Jerusalem."*

Everything about Him is lovely. He is the King without sin and the God who died. She knows everything that comes out of His mouth is good, even when He says "woe" to the Pharisees. When she cannot understand the meaning of His words, she has confidence that everything He says is good because He is love, holy, just, and good.

He is not only her lover. He is her friend. In a happy marriage, the partners are not only lovers. They are friends. There are marriages where the partners are only lovers. These soon tire of one another. Other marriages are only friends. To be friends is good, but an important element is missing. He is both lover and friend to her. She experiences the fullness of relationship. She also does not hesitate to tell others of this because they can enjoy this relationship as well.

Song 6:1 "Where has your lover gone, most beautiful of women? Which way did your lover turn, that we may look for him with you?"

Her description of Him caused them to want to search for Him. Speaking forth the attributes of the Bridegroom has that effect. Though we try by many methods to excite the people of God, only this method works to bring true devotion. If we will know Him and make Him known, the church will grow up into maturity. The church will desire Him, as He deserves to be desired. No gimmicks are needed; just a life that is His. Our cheerleading tactics and programs to get His people involved will not do it. They only prolong His coming. If we make Him, the center of everything, we will see the bride arise in glory. He will not come until she is ready.

In the Bridal Garden

Song 6:2 *"My lover has gone down to his garden, to the beds of spices, to browse in the gardens and to gather lilies."*

His garden is His bride. He has gone to His people. He is among those who have beds of spices. What does this mean? The perfection of the bride is a corporate perfection. Though to study Song of Songs, it is necessary to look at the individual relationship; the bride is a corporate people. No one of us will be perfect. That would be to say we become gods. That which I lack in perfection my neighbor has. When the Lord looks at His bride, He sees us perfect because of His blood. He also sees this because corporately we are whole. Every gift and grace are represented in the bride. If we try to be perfect on our own, we will only fall into error, perfectionism, or frustration.

To these He has gone. The lilies *(Song 2)* are the insignificant ones who have come out of slavery and still have the voices of the slaveholders ringing in their ears. He gathers them to Himself and He will not let them slip out of His hand. He is among the hurting people He loves. The bride shares Him with other hurting members of the bride because she knows that is the only road to fulfillment and love.

Take Me

Take that which is crushed and bring your sweetness.
Take that which is broken and shine your light.
Take that which is poured out
 And heal your beloved.
Take me.
All of me,
I give to you.

For Reflection

1. What would you say to seekers that shows them He is better than others? How could you help them see His beauty?

2. Ask the Lord to present you with an opportunity to share with someone what you see in Him.

3. Why could focus on the cost keep you from knowing Him intimately?

4. How can you avoid focusing on the cost now and the pain of that cost when it comes? What scriptures could you memorize to help you?

5. How does the description in Song of Songs compare to the descriptions below, and how are they different?

Ex. 24:10 "and saw the God of Israel. Under his feet was something like a pavement made of sapphire, clear as the sky itself."

Ezek. 10:1 "I looked, and I saw the likeness of a throne of sapphire above the expanse that was over the heads of the cherubim."

Ezek. 1:26 "Above the expanse over their heads was what looked like a throne of sapphire, and high above on the throne was a figure like that of a man." Read all of Eze.1 for a better look.

6. Does your life inspire others to seek hard after Him?

Prayer

Lord, help me see you as the Bridegroom glorified. I want to know your strength, your grace, and your unfathomable love. Show me the path that leads directly into your presence and heart. Draw me so I will learn to run after you. Open my eyes that I will see you as the Lamb who was slain, the Lord among the golden candlesticks of Revelation and the only one worthy to open the seals of the scroll.

I need to know you as the one who comes to spend time with me, who desires to see my face and hear my voice. Show me the path to your presence. Remove from me all that keeps me from coming. Then help me describe you to the other members of the bride that they will desire you more than life. Send me out with your glory blazing from my life. Show yourself gloriously in me.

Chapter 19

City of Warriors

Delightsome City

Song 6:4 "You are beautiful, my darling, as Tirzah, lovely as Jerusalem, majestic as troops with banners."

The bride failed when she fell into complacency. She was avoiding conflict. Her life was full of past conflict. There was enough resisting the enemy's plan and purpose. She fought enough battles. Because of this attitude, He roused her out of her slumber then left to make her hunger for Him. Out of this came a wonderful ministry to others that they will love Him. How does the Bridegroom see her now after her complacency? Is she in disgrace?

The word Tirzah means delightsome. Tirzah was a city in the northern kingdom of Israel. This city was so beautiful people named it delightsome. It was also to become the capital of Israel in later years due to its location. Tirzah was set on a hill. Cities set on hills have an advantage in times of warfare.

Matthew 5:14 "You are the light of the world. A city on a hill cannot be hidden. Neither do people light a lamp and put it under a bowl."

Once she was content to be the light hidden under the bowl. A light under a bowl is not light since no one can see it. Without oxygen, it goes out. Yet now she is the city set on the hill. She has strategic advantage in time of battle because she is declaring Him. It was her previous declaration of Him to the friends that has made this description of her possible. Coming out of complacency, she has learned that beautiful cities get attacked because people want what those cities have. The purpose of setting a city on a hill is to see the enemy when he comes and to have strategic superiority during battle. She is the city. His people are the city. She is set on the hill because He loves her. This is not a matter of choice. It is a fact. She must watch, ever a watchman, so the enemy's attack would not be a surprise. Preparedness brings victory in battle. Complacency brings defeat.

He speaks again of her beauty when He compares her to Jerusalem. *Revelation 21:9b-11a* '"Come I will show you the bride, the wife of the Lamb." And he carried me away in the Spirit to a mountain great and high, and showed me the Holy City, Jerusalem, coming down out of heaven from God. It shone with the glory of God..."'

When He speaks to His wife of being lovely as Jerusalem, He sees the bride as a company of people, a city and an individual. When He looks at her, the glory of God covers her. She is beautiful because she is chosen, prepared, set apart, and obedient. Her beauty exists because of His presence. *Revelation 21:22-23 "I did not see a temple in the city because the Lord God Almighty and the Lamb are its temple. The city does not need the sun or the moon to shine on it, for the glory of God gives it light, and the Lamb is its lamp."*

This picture of the bride is not just for a future day. He sees her this way now. Believers can take part in as much or as little as they desire. Some walk close to God. When they pass from this earth and become a part of the heavenly Jerusalem, there is little difference for them. There are others to whom heaven is a shock. The lives of those who walk close to God can be touched in lasting ways because of His presence. The one who walks with God challenges others to know Him, too. Those who walk close to God will have many crowns to lie at His feet. The bride lives to honor Him with those crowns and with her life.

An Army

This next description in Song 6:4 is military, "majestic as troops with banners". The banner is the standard of the King that goes before the army into battle. It rouses the hearts of the army to be brave and fight well. The flag challenges those who are staying at home to be supportive of the army. The standard is a sign to the enemy of the power of the king. Our King's flag is love. For example, picture the corporate bride in the earth. Millions strong, she marches forward with flag after flag on which is emblazoned the word love. Perhaps His nail-pierced hands are upon one flag and on another we see the crown of thorns. On another would be a slain lamb. These show forth His love. This is the army that wins the battle of all battles. The King of Love and the Bride of His heart will win it.

Much happened to bring the bride to this day. Complacency was an inevitable step along the way to becoming a militant bride ready to battle at the slightest command. Complacency was inevitable because after fierce battles, we believe we deserve a rest.

Song 6:5 "Turn your eyes from me, they overwhelm me." Overwhelm means, "to act stormily ".xxxv These are the eyes He sees. Her eyes take Him by storm. Are you surprised that this description is of you?

Cease Striving

Psa. 46:10 "Be still and know that I am God." Many believers are performance based. Even though we believe in the rest of God, we live in a constant state of manic performance. *Psa. 46:10* was written for us.

When by habit or neurotic pattern we rush, we are shutting Him out of circumstances. If we are acting, He cannot. If we rest in Him and do only as we see Him doing, then the results are His action and will in our world. One thing is sure, we cannot know what He is doing if we are always rushing.

This bride, once complacent, is now full of courage; high-spirited, she attacks. She is a warrior who expects to fight and rises to the challenge. Her rest is in His presence. She fights within the protection of His presence. Her fight is from a position of rest rather than manic performance. When He looks at her, this still warrior is what He sees. No wonder He is overwhelmed.

Song 6:8-9 "Sixty queens, there may be, and eighty concubines, and virgins beyond number; but my dove, my perfect one, is unique, the only daughter of her mother, the favorite of the one who bore her."

No other that compares to her. She is one of a kind, the only daughter of her mother the church. There will only be one bride. The Lord is using a poetic structure to let us know she is "it". In Solomon's day, there were many queens, concubines and virgins without number, but there was only one beloved bride. In the heart of our heavenly Solomon others are as nothing compared to the only bride He desires. He gave His life to win her.

According to this verse she is perfect, unique, and only. The word perfect means blameless in the original Hebrew.xxxvi

Ephesians 5:27 "For he chose us in him before the creation of the world, to be holy and blameless in his sight."

I Peter 2:9 "But you are a chosen people, a royal priesthood, a holy nation, a people belonging to God, that you may declare the praises of him who called you out of darkness into his wonderful light."

She was chosen in Him before He created man. He chose her to be holy and blameless in His sight. Note that the Holiness is "in His sight". It is the way He views her because He sees her through His blood. To be chosen does not mean to reach perfection in this life. The perfection that she carries is His attributes at work in her.

He has called her to purpose. She is to declare His praises and tell of her journey from darkness to light. She is pressing into His presence and that brings with it a pressing into His purpose.

Perfect one means separated. She separated herself from the things of this life as He separated Himself unto the Father when He walked among us.

The Army Again

Song 6:*10 "Who is this that appears like the dawn, fair as the moon, bright as the sun, majestic as the stars in procession."*

The friends of the bride describe her this way. The prior verse said the queens and concubines praised her. This is that praise.

They compare her to the moon that shines at night. During the night seasons, she shines forth to give light to others.

She is also compared to the sun. So was the Lord. In *Matthew 17:2, and Revelation 1:16* His face was said to shine like the sun. This is a picture of the glory of God. *Judges 5:31 "So may all your enemies perish, O Lord! But may all who love you be like the sun when it rises in its strength."*

This is a picture of the glory of God upon His bride. The city does not need the light of the moon or the sun for the Lamb is its lamp *(Rev. 21)*. The Bridegroom's friends view the bride this way.

There is something else they see also. Though the NIV renders this passage, *"majestic as the stars in procession,"* the KJV renders it *"terrible as an army with banners"*. The truth is the word army is not in the text. This literally reads, terrible with banners. If she is terrible and has banners, she is being compared to an army. Thus, the word army was added to the text in the KJV.

The friends see her ability to shine in the night during the darkest difficulties. They see the glory of the Bridegroom upon her bringing the full light of day to dispel the darkness. And they see her as a bannered host that can bring destruction upon the kingdoms of darkness. She is ready, willing, and able to battle the enemy of the souls of His people and win. Her principal weapons are prayer, worship, obedience. and the word of God. Many talk about us being the army of God. Often songs are sung of victories won.

If we are a victorious people, we are a suffering people. Intercession is work. Obedience costs us everything we think is important. Standing in the truth when every circumstance screams, the opposite is hard. To be a warrior is to suffer the bitter agony of lost skirmishes while we learn. It is difficult to hear His voice in the thick of the battle. The confusion of the battle keeps us from implementing that which we hear. Therefore, we must study His word. We must prevail and win for the Lord that for which He suffered. We must become skilled in warfare and learn to hear His voice and obey in every circumstance.

Song 6:11 *"I went down to the grove of nut trees to look at the new growth in the valley to see if the vines had budded or the pomegranates were in bloom."*

The NIV attributes this speech to the Bridegroom; other translations attribute it to the bride. We will look at it from the bride's point of view.

This garden has the first growth after winter, as evidenced by nut trees that have carried their fruit over the winter and recent growth, which comes at the first sign of spring. During the days of complacency, fruitfulness was nonexistent. That is a winter season. But a new day has dawned with her renewed love for Him. Once again, fruitfulness is budding within her life. She shared with others who He is, and they desired Him. She looks to see if that seed is budding. Has the vine brought forth fruit? Will there be a new revelation of the wine of His blood among His people?

Are the pomegranates blooming? Will there be a harvest of righteousness among them?

Song 6:12 Before I realized it my desire set me among the royal chariots of my people. NASB.

12 Before I was aware, my soul set me
Over the chariots of my noble people. NAS.

The words noble people in the New American Standard means my willing people, or volunteers (as a soldier). Her soul sets her among them. She is following the instructions of the Lord. His will has become her will in new ways.

As a result, she finds herself among the people of the Lord who are willing volunteers. They are in chariots. They are an army. She finds herself among the army as she goes to do what needs to be done. These are the intercessors.

His people are willing volunteers because He was the ultimate willing volunteer. By laying down His life willingly He fought the greatest battle of all time.

The Encampment

Song 6:13 "Come back, come back, O Shulamite; come back that we may *gaze upon you."*

These daughters of Jerusalem need to know Him, and the bride has a ministry to perform in showing Him forth unto them. The Bride cannot stay forever in the presence of those who volunteer for the army. She must go to those still in slavery and love and encourage them. She must uphold those who are in the tomb that they do not grow weary and lose heart.

Now the Lover speaks. Song 6:13b "Why should you gaze on the Shulamite as on the dance of Mahanaim?"

The root word for Mahanaim means an encampment, army of dancers, soldiers etc. [xxxvii] *This refers to Genesis 32:1-2 "Jacob also went on his way and the angels of God met him. When Jacob saw them he said, "This is the camp of God!" So, he named that place Mahanaim."* Jacob was going to meet Esau. The Lord's troops met Jacob's army, and they formed one army.

The bride is not alone in her battles. This army includes warriors and angels.

Rev. 8:1 "When the Lamb broke the seventh seal, there was silence in heaven for about half an hour.

Rev. 8:2 And I saw the seven angels who stand before God, and seven trumpets were given to them.

Rev. 8:3 Another angel came and stood at the altar, holding a golden censer; and much incense was given to him, so that he might add it to the prayers of all the saints on the golden altar which was before the throne.

Rev. 8:4 And the smoke of the incense, with the prayers of the saints, went up before God out of the angel's hand.

Rev. 8:5 Then the angel took the censer and filled it with the fire of the altar and threw it to the earth; and there followed peals of thunder and sounds and flashes of lightning and an earthquake.

Rev. 8:6 And the seven angels who had the seven trumpets prepared themselves to sound them." NASB

The prayers, worship, and warfare of the bride is mixed with the incense of heaven and is thrown to earth bringing last day's judgments *(Rev. 5:1 to 6:1)* What is coming is the revelation of Jesus Christ, the coming forth of the Bridegroom Lamb and the perfecting of His bride. Only the Lamb is worthy to bring these last judgments. The heart of the bride so longs for her beloved that her prayers and longing contribute to the final chapter of history. *Revelation 17* tells us that Babylon, the Mother of Harlots and the beast will make war against the Lamb. The bride's prayers will help bring the final judgment on these.

Rev. 17:14 *"These will wage war against the Lamb, and the Lamb will overcome them, because He is Lord of lords and King of kings, and those who are with Him are the called and chosen and faithful." NASB.*

The army of God is an army of prayers. Wherever we see the Harlot, the bride does not capitulate. She trusts in the Bridegroom Lamb. The bride wars against the deceptions ensnaring others.

The Harlot's Destruction

She is also called to the prayer and warfare that will bring the harlot's final judgment. Revelation 8 shows this truth.

Revelation 18:1 begins the story of the harlot's demise.

Rev. 18:4 *"I heard another voice from heaven, saying, "Come out of her, my people, so that you will not participate in her sins and receive of her plagues; "NASB.*

This verse tells us it is possible for "my people" to be in the harlot. This is the biggest part of the bride's ministry, calling His people out of the Harlot. The Lamb wants everyone to join Him and reflect His glory in the earth rather than seeking their own. The harlot rewards those who seek their own glory and their own fulfillment, and she masquerades as the church and the bride. In Jesus day, the harlot church, the pharisaical system crucified Him. The harlot church persecutes the Bride and believes it does God a favor.

In scripture, birds foul things and are often a type of demonic ownership. In the passage below we are told that Babylon is a dwelling place of demons, unclean spirits and unclean birds because the nations have drunk the wine of the passion of her immorality.

Rev. 18:1 "After these things I saw another angel coming down from heaven, having great authority, and the earth was illumined with his glory.

Rev. 18:2 And he cried out with a mighty voice, saying, "Fallen, fallen is Babylon the great! She has become a dwelling place of demons and a prison of every unclean spirit, and a prison of every unclean and hateful bird.

Rev. 18:3 "For all the nations have drunk of the wine of the passion of her immorality, and the kings of the earth have committed acts of immorality with her, and the merchants of the earth have become rich by the wealth of her sensuality." NASB.

This means that the nations trusted in something besides the Lord for provision and life. Immorality is adultery against God. Even the church is involved in this. The Harlot is the economic, political and religious systems of the world. *(Rev 18:1-24)*

Babylon is a city. So is the bride. We will look at the bride city in later chapters.

Cities contain many people. Babylon has many participants. These participants go to work (commerce and finance) worship (even atheists worship their system of belief) and are governed (politics). In her was found the blood of saints and prophets.

This warfare is serious and brings life or death spiritually. The bride "gets" this and understands that the stakes are high. She looks to the King. She watches the longing in His eyes for more to join her. So, she works and prays and encourages and shines His glory no matter the cost. His longing motivates her.

There is a dance of Mahanaim. This is a showing of public exaltation for joy. The bride and the angels of God are giving a show in the earth. It is a dance of the triumph of the Lamb.

Victory is assured since the Lord already won on Calvary. But the dance must continue until the end, until He comes again and destroys the last enemy, death. When He comes, the battle will be done for eternity. For now, we are to occupy until He comes.

The Warrior Bride

From slave to warrior
she rises in glory
no allegiance to men
a soldier in the field
a company of people
winning victories
for the Lamb of God.

The Dancer

Once men would say dance dancer dance.
She danced and served and served and danced.
Joy was not in the dance, not in the slave's dance.

Now she is set free to dance for the King,
set free from hard servitude.

Dance dancer dance.
Dance with joy,
the joy of the bride,
not the obligation of the slave.

Dance dancer dance,
there are victories to be won,
for the King of love.

Dance dancer dance,
listen to the great choreographer

and dance the dance He has written for you.
No other dance will do.

As you dance before His love banner
the enemy is pushed back.
he cannot withstand your beauty.
he cannot overcome your joy.
he cannot stop your love.

Your feet dance on the high places of the earth.
You scale the places that other feet cannot go.
You are being watched by those
who cannot believe you would be so loved.
They want to know that what you know,
is possible.

So, dance dancer dance and win for your Love
the desire of His heart.
The company of dancers in the earth
that shine like the sun.

For Reflection:

1. Read *Hebrew 3:7-4:13* Ask the Lord how you need to enter His rest and what it would look like to war from that place of rest? Write down what He says.

2. What 3 steps could you take today to move more fully into His presence and will?

3. What do you need to do to love the Lord to the point of total obedience?

4. Picture yourself as His beautiful bride dancing before the army. It is a dance that He shows you as you move forward. As you twirl and dip, the enemy flees. You are the bride of the Lamb, moving in the authority He has

and dancing His victory into place. You know which move to make because you are dancing His dance. Hear each move directly from His mouth. Now dance!

Prayer

Lord, how foolish I have been to hang back from warfare. How foolish I have been to not understand that warfare is connected to your heart and purposes. Help me dance the dance that brings your hand to bear upon situations in the earth. Help me dip and twirl, glide and scoop according to your choreography. It is your dance. Show me the moves that will set others free.

Help those who view the dance to see that you are ALL and it is your dance, your glory. May we see the victory only you bring. Show us who you are as the King of Kings and Lord of Lords, as the Lamb, as the Bridegroom. Open our hearts to grasp what you are calling us to, so we will never lose the understanding of our bride hood and your place as our Bridegroom.

Chapter 20

The Dancer

The Dance

This next description of the bride shows the one who performs the dance of two armies until every enemy is put under the Lord's feet. Again, the bride is presented as a corporate people. This is evidenced by the earlier verse showing the coming together of the two armies. Here is individual application as well.

The first description of the bride in Chapter Four is of her fidelity and Christ likeness. She is described from the top of her head to her breasts. This picture was of the joy set before Him when He endured the cross.

The second description in Chapter Six only spoke of her head. This shows her new way of thinking. Not only is she no longer a slave, but she also no longer thinks like one either. She experienced the renewal of her mind from that of a slave to an intercessor, a warrior.

An intercessor first conquers the enemies that attack their lives, then they pray for others. Those who try to conquer demonic kingdoms when those kingdoms still reign in their own minds experience frustration and failure. Therefore, we see our warrior's head to let us know, with a renewal of the mind, the warrior is ready.

The Bride with Wholeness

This description of the bride shows the whole bride. The bride has spiritual children. She is presented as a company more often. As we slay the dragons in our lives and experience renewal of our minds, we become a united army. However, if we believe the lies of the enemy, those lies will separate us from the Lord and one another. How will we draw close to God when we accept lies about Him? How can we show love to His people if we are not drawing close to Him? We cannot affect change that will help others overcome the deception in their lives if we stay in denial and deception about the root of our own problems,.

Song 7:1 "How beautiful your sandaled feet, O prince's daughter."

Romans 10:15 'And how can they preach unless they are sent. As it is written, "How beautiful are the feet of them that bring good news."

Part of the dance she must dance is to bring the good news gospel to the people. Her feet are sandaled; they are *"fitted with the readiness that comes from the gospel of peace." (Ephesians 6:15)* The gospel of peace is more than the initial truth of salvation through His blood. Salvation is good news, but there is more good news. We can enjoy a relationship with Him. He is knowable. He wants to speak to His people. The gospel is about Him. Wherever she walks, she shows, speaks and lives the gospel.

Once she didn't want to soil her feet to reach others because of complacency. Now she walks as the daughter of the Prince. She is royalty and works for the good of His kingdom.

The word prince is the same word in Chapter Six verse twelve. It means willing or voluntary. He was the volunteer, and she is His daughter. Thus, her work is voluntary. At one time, she did not understand His sacrifice or His ways. She feared His plan for her will be bad. Now she has learned of His love and volunteers. She does not minister under compulsion, but out of relationship.

Song 7:1b "Your graceful legs are like jewels, the work of a craftsman's hands."

Genesis 32:25 "When the man saw that he could not overpower him he touched the socket of Jacob's hip so that his hip was wrenched as he wrestled."

The leg is a sign of strength. When the angel wrestled with Jacob, he touched his strength. The usurper, Jacob, became the man who limped when he walked. God changed his walk. The bride had her walk changed by the dealings of God. The craftsman was the Lord. He touched her in the thigh and changed her walk. Whatever was in her of the usurper is gone and, in its place, is one who leads others into God's presence.

Song 7:2 "Your navel is a rounded goblet that never lacks blended wine. Your waist is a mound of wheat encircled by lilies."

The navel in scripture is the center of strength. In her center of strength, is the wine of His blood. She has strength in her center because He is there. This is spiced wine. That is a picture of His suffering and death. The spices result from sharing in the fellowship of His sufferings.

Her belly, in this description, resembles a heap of wheat. The wheat is a picture of His body given for us, and the sustaining power of His word. This is likewise at the center of her strength. Her strength is not her own. The power that we see in her is His sustaining.

This heaped belly is lost muscle tone because of childbirth. She is a mother in Israel. The lilies are his people. Spiritual children gathered round her center of strength from which they came. Her childbearing capacities reveal the broken bread and the poured-out wine. Her spiritual children gather round these symbols of the Love of her life.

There is something else included here. *Ephesians 6:14* *"Stand firm then, with the belt of truth buckled round your waist..."* The belly is the area upon which the belt of truth is worn, and the high priest wore the girdle. Similarly, she wears her armor. She is the warrior bride. Her preparedness for battle is constant. She is ready for any emergency. She functions as a priest before the Lord. Her communion with Him is direct. There is no intermediary.

Ministry

Song 7:3 "Your breasts are like two fawns, twins of a gazelle."

Again, the breasts represent ministry. The gazelle shows she birthed ministry out of the glory of God. There is another picture as well. The breastplate of the High Priest was double, *Exodus 39:9*. This breastplate enabled the High Priest to get answers from God. This is a picture of hearing the Lord, so ministry comes from God. The bride ministers out of His glory. She cannot see His glory or hear Him aside from His presence. Thus, the breasts depict the hearing bride and the nurturing and ministering bride.

The New Testament speaks of a breastplate. It is the breastplate of righteousness, *Ephesians 6:14*. She goes forth with the breastplate of His righteousness into battle. His blood, His sacrifice protects her.

Song 7:4 "Your neck is like an ivory tower."

The neck is again a watchtower. Ivory is a representation of purity and beauty. Ivory was only affordable to royalty and the wealthy. She is the bride of the King.

The watchtower was important in ancient times. A guard on the tower warned of the approaching enemy and gave time to prepare for war. The bride is vigilant in seeing the enemy and giving warning at His approach. Others have the enemy controlling their lives, but the mature bride resists and fights every inroad of the enemy.

Song 4: b "Your eyes are the pools of Heshbon by the gate of Bath Rabbim."

A pool collects water. It is still and deep. The bride has the living water within her. It is His water. The bride is not alarmed by what she sees happening around her. Her waters are not churned. There is peace and stillness within her. Similarly, there is depth. Full of His living water, she is not content with surface relationship. She lives her life to know Him in the fullest sense possible.

The name Bath Rabbim means daughter of a multitude. xxxviii She is one of many. We see the corporate bride. The gate is the place of leadership and authority in the ancient city. The bride walks with her King's authority. Amid the multitude of her people, she has peace. It's amazing, especially considering she's vigilant for the enemy as a warrior. When we are subject to the enemy, the ease we enjoy is false. Many feel vigilance in warfare and prayer is too much. The tyranny of the enemies' lies is far more difficult. We find the path to real peace in the process Song of Songs portrays. In fact, the mature bride is a warrior who lives in peace even during the most difficult circumstances.

Song 7:4c "Your nose is like the tower of Lebanon looking toward Damascus."

Again, we have a watchtower. Notice the scripture illustrating the peaceful pools is couched between two descriptions of watchtowers. If ever there was biblical proof, that warfare is to be a natural state of life, this verse contains it. To those who attempt to attain peace without warfare against the enemy and much intercession to God, this tells us it will not happen. You cannot have the true peace of God without reckoning with the enemy of our souls. You may have complacency or laziness, but you will not have the peace that comes from being intimately related to Him. That intimacy depends on the plans and purposes of the enemy being overturned within the life. That is the beginning.

This refers to Damascus because David conquered Syria. In Solomon's day, Damascus became free of Israeli rule. Their new enemy is seen best from the Tower of Lebanon.

The bride learns warfare and war strategy by experience. Some feel the only way to pray, or war, is by divine revelation. In contrast, when trouble comes, the bride learns what works and what does not. The other element is God's voice. Yes, He speaks in her heart and lets her know what she must do. Yes, He quickens prayer by the Spirit within her for others. However, the part experience plays in her life is equally important.

Using the nose as a tower is humorous. Have you ever heard it said, "I could smell them coming?" That is the picture here. After many battles, the bride senses, or "smells," the enemy. It is part experience and part the voice of the Lord, but she knows before anyone sees it. Others think she is crazy, but with the mature bride, what she senses will prove so.

There is no substitute for experience. It took many years and much difficulty to sense the enemy before he reveals himself. The bride is not a lazy person. She is active in her seeking of the Lord, active in finding wholeness, and active in seeking the utmost good of His people.

Mind of Christ

Song 7:5 "Your head crowns you like Mount Carmel. xxxix Your hair is like royal tapestry; the king is held captive by its tresses."

Carmel means fruitful field, park, or garden. The bride's mind is fruitful. She has the mind of Christ.

Romans 12:2-3 "Do not conform any longer to the pattern of this world but be transformed by the renewing of your mind. Then you will be able to test and approve what God's will is."

When she said no to slavery, she stopped conforming. Likewise, when she said yes to leave the tomb, she again stopped conforming to the world's pattern. She said a resounding no when she quit conforming to the enemy's lies.

Old Self, New Self

Ephesians 4:22-25 "You were taught with regard to your former way of life to put off your old self, which is being corrupted by its desires; to be made new in the attitude of your minds, and to put on the new self, created to be like God in true righteousness and holiness."

The old self is being corrupted by its desires. It is that self to which she said no. The word renews our minds and enables us to put on the new self. Our bride studies the word and challenges the "old self" thoughts.

The picture of her hair like a royal tapestry has the colors of purple for His kingship, red for His blood, and white for His purity. Her hair is the covering of the renewed mind. These colors indicate the veil into the Holy of Holies. Her mind is fruitful because she subjects it to Him and because she communes with Him intimately beyond the veil in the Holy of Holies. Seeing the lie is the first step, but that seeing is useless without the intimacy. The renewed mind cannot come by seeing alone. In time, something must replace the lies. That replacement happens in communion with the Lord. Both things together create the renewed mind.

This is so wonderful to the Lord that He is held captive by her hair. That suggests He wants to be with her. That He cannot leave her even as a captive will be constrained to stay. Intimacy with the Lord is available to every believer. He wants us to know Him in the depths of our being. He wants us to hold Him captive by our subjection and loving communion.

The story of Elijah on Mount Carmel shows another picture of the bride's renewed mind *(I Ki. 18)*. It was on Mount Carmel that Elijah slew the prophets of Baal. The bride said no to the enemy and put to death the false prophets, the false voices. This is something else the Lord sees when He compares her head to Carmel.

His Delight

Song 7:6 "How beautiful you are and how pleasing, O love, with your delights!"

No wonder this verse in included. She is beautiful, pleasing and delightful. The last verse showed such a wonderful truth about her. He had to stop here in this verse to savor the wonder of it. The intimacy He knows with the people of the bride, with you, is beyond description. "Delights", is the word He uses to describe what she brings to Him. Delights speak of intimacy at a level we cannot fully understand until we are with Him forever.

Her Fruitfulness

Song 7:7 "Your *stature is like that of the palm, and your breasts like clusters of fruit."*

The bride is tall and straight; she has no crookedness in her. Stature refers not only to height but also quality or status gained by growth. This is her true stature. The quality developed in her is like the stature of the palm. A palm tree bends in the wind without breaking. The bride has learned to bend in the winds of adversity and not break. This tree bears fruit in old age. Likewise, the bride is fruitful, for her mind is fruitful. The glory of God upon her will cause spiritual children to be born, even in her old age. The palm has long taproots that find water during dryness. She has known many dry seasons and sent her roots deep into the waters of God. Even though she stands in a desert region, she thrives, for she has found the Lord to be enough.

Comparing her breasts to clusters of fruit shows the abundant fruitfulness of her life. The success of the taproot nourishing the tree in a desert place is shown in this passage. She has clusters of fruit. Fruitfulness does not depend on location, but the source of the nourishment. The Lord and His words are nourishment indeed.

Song 7:8 'I said, "I will climb the palm tree; I will take hold of its fruit." May your breasts be like the clusters of the vine.'

When someone wants to get to the fruit of the date palm, they put a large strap around the tree and their own body. Then they crawl to the top, using the strap to keep them from falling. There would only be two reasons for doing this since it is dangerous, to get the palm leaves or to harvest fruit. When the Bridegroom sees the fruitfulness of the bride, He desires to sample the fruit. The dates hang in clusters like grapes, thus the reference to clusters of the vine.

The fruitfulness of the bride is available because of His life within her. She cannot take credit for this. She said yes to God each step of the way. We only proceed by saying yes one step at a time. It's not everything, but it's enough.

Song 7:8b "the fragrance of your breath like apples."

Her breath smells like apples because she is receiving the harvest of the one fruit tree, Song 2:3. As she feeds on His fruit, her breath carries the smell of Him wherever she goes. This is a picture of His Indwelling Holy Spirit within her speaking forth from her life.

Her Wine Is For Him

Song *7:9 "and your mouth like the best wine."*

This one who God dealt with speaks forth blessing. There is life within her that flows out when she speaks. At Cana of Galilee, the best wine was served last. In the end times the bride will have a greater anointing than before. The blessing that comes forth from her life will be the best yet. His church will come into a fuller knowledge of Him because the days demand it. The bride will experience the fullest blessing of knowing Him and will speak forth His glory in the earth.

Song 7:9b "May the wine go straight to my lover, flowing gently over lips and teeth."

This is the bride speaking. This fruitfulness is for Him. What others receive is the natural result of a life turned toward

Him. Likewise, there is no ambition in ministry, no bringing forth a mighty anointing, or a new truth. The bride dwells in His presence, causing fruitfulness, which she delights in for His sake, not her acceptance or popularity. This fruitfulness cannot help flowing from her life to touch others, but her motive is to please Him alone. Ministry for her is a response of love unto Him.

The word teeth are most often rendered sleepers; thus, this would most likely read as follows. The wine goes first to the Lord. Then it flows to those who are asleep to waken them to love of the Bridegroom. The bride's mission is to know Him and make Him known. The wine, the fruitfulness of her garden goes to Him. This means knowing Him in intimate fellowship. Then the overflow of that relationship makes Him known. Self-effort in ministry is dead, and she is alive to Him in a way that shows Him to the world. She does not need evangelistic methods to make Him known. She needs Him. This devotion touches the sleepers.

These passages show the dancer that He sees. She dances the dance of two armies, the Church and the Heavenly Host. He spoke to her what He sees in her, and she replies in the next verse.

True Love

Song 7:10 "I belong to my lover, and his desire is for me."

The bride's idea of love in the beginning was a romantic fantasy. "My lover belongs to me." This is not true love speaking. It is a romantic ideal. It is rejoicing that we have someone to love. In human relationships, this is dangerous because the result of this is an attempt to change the lover into what a romantic ideal that looks like to us. When this happens in a marriage, the results are disastrous. An ideal exists only in the imagination. In fact, when we see the Lord as a romantic ideal we are in danger. He does not change. That means we must. We must change our ideal and choose the truth about who He is.

The individual who has learned this lesson knows a sense of belonging. We love only because He first loved us. He belongs to us because we first belonged to Him. His desire is for His bride. Until the bride learns this truth, she is resisting the will of God because she wants to change that will, thereby changing Him to fit her theology.

The bride company will see, love and know Him. Their hearts will sing, *"I belong to my lover, and his desire is for me."* They know the love of the Bridegroom in its truth and glory. Because of this, they will be a force in the earth. The day we live in demands it.

This description is of the dancer He died to purchase. He invites us all to be that dancer. Have you accepted the invitation? Will you accept it now?

Hear the rejoicing over the Harlot's demise and the readiness of the bride:

Rev. 19:1 'After these things I heard something like a loud voice of a great multitude in heaven, saying, "Hallelujah! salvation and glory and power belong to our God;

Rev. 19:2 BECAUSE HIS JUDGMENTS ARE TRUE AND RIGHTEOUS; for He has judged the great harlot who was corrupting the earth with her immorality, and HE HAS AVENGED THE BLOOD OF HIS BOND-SERVANTS ON HER."

Rev. 19:3 And a second time they said, "Hallelujah! HER SMOKE RISES UP FOREVER AND EVER."

Rev. 19:4 And the twenty-four elders and the four living creatures fell down and worshiped God who sits on the throne saying, "Amen. Hallelujah!"

Rev. 19:5 And a voice came from the throne, saying, "Give praise to our God, all you His bond-servants, you who fear Him, the small and the great."

Rev. 19:6 Then I heard something like the voice of a great multitude and like the sound of many waters and like the sound of mighty peals of thunder, saying, "Hallelujah! For the Lord our God, the Almighty, reigns.

Rev. 19:7 "Let us rejoice and be glad and give the glory to Him, for the marriage of the Lamb has come and His bride has made herself ready.

Rev. 19:8 It was given to her to clothe herself in fine linen, bright and clean; for the fine linen is the righteous acts of the saints.

Rev. 19:9 Then he *said to me, "Write, 'Blessed are those who are invited to the marriage supper of the Lamb.'" And he *said to me, "These are true words of God." NASB.

There is a bride in the earth that has "made herself ready". She has received her garments from the King. She learned to dance the army dance. Because of her, many have joined the company of the bride. Because of her, the Harlot is judged. She is in the company of the dancers of Mahanaim. The two armies, the army of God and the bride company, are as one. She no longer wonders how to approach her Lover since she is always close to Him. Her every movement is made with His direction. They dance, He leads, and she follows. See her dance in the earth with Him at the lead.

Glorious Dancer Bride

Glorious dancer bride
what makes you dance?
Dancing by the pools of Heshbon
resting in His depths.

Warrior?… dancer?… bride?
How can you be all of these?

"The King of Love has called me to dance.
He it is that has called me
To rest in the depths of Him
who is the pool of rest.
I dance in the presence of
the One who calls me to His heart.
There is no mystery to the dance.
There is only Him, Lord of the Dance
calling me to come
loving me to dance.

He leads
I follow.
I dance for Him.
I dive deep into His pool
and rest in His depths..

He is my strength.
He is my delight.
He is my breath.
He is my depth.
There is none other."

For Reflection:

1. Have you accepted His invitation to the depths? If not, what holds you back?
2. What will you do today to move deeper into Him?
3. Can you smell the enemy coming? Would you like to know how? Ask Him to show you what this means for you.
4. Write what the palm tree's description means to you.
5. Is there any part of the picture of the palm tree that you are lacking? Should that be true, seek the Lord's guidance in understanding the area where you lack and how to embody that quality.
6. What are you speaking in the earth? Is it spoken with the breath of the Bridegroom Lamb? Is it His glory? If not His glory, ask Him to show you how you must change what you say. Seek Him until you have his answer and write your impressions.

Prayer

My Lord and my King, my pool of rest and refreshing, I come to you. There is no other place of rest, no other depth that refreshes me. I have so often gone to other pools that the world offers. I have gone to the pools of entertainment and the pools of men's ideas. Help me turn to you and learn to rest only in you. Draw my heart to the dance you have created for me to dance. May my beauty overwhelm you because of your image in me? Let me embody the palm tree that remains fruitful and resilient through any storm. I pray you will be drawn to the fruitfulness that comes from me resting in you. Help me understand that your desire is for me.

Slay every lie that says I am not enough. Through your blood, I am everything you desire. By your righteousness, I am your chosen. In you everything you have envisioned for me will be done.

I bow at your feet, my God, who gives me breath. Here is my bowed heart and my body. I rend my heart and my garment and give you my life again. It is not possible to give too much. Keep me from giving too little. Help me give my life as a living sacrifice daily, take up my cross daily, and glorify you daily. Reveal your great glory and transform me. Be glorified in me ...at last.

Chapter 21

Insignificance

Fruitfulness in Ministry

Song 7:11 "Come, my lover, let us go to the countryside, let us spend the night in the villages."

The bride knows her calling, and she invites the Bridegroom to come with her to the places of ministry. It is now unthinkable to minister without Him.

To many, the countryside is insignificant. A village is unimportant; the city or town is a much larger hub of activity. Likewise, that mentality has invaded the church. Bigger is not better. The bride wants to go to the insignificant ones, to the ones often overlooked by the church power brokers of our day. She and the Bridegroom plan to spend the night with the unimportant. The night speaks of the difficulty believers face. Though many in the church esteem the rich or the powerful as better, the mature bride does not. In fact, she has a heart for the lowest in man's eyes. She and the Lord go to these in difficulty to help and encourage them and to see their progress.

Song 7:12 "Let us go early to the vineyards to see if their vines have budded, if their blossoms have opened, and if the pomegranates are in bloom - there, I will give you my love."

Early suggests an urgency to get the job started. The bride learned her lesson well. She knows that by loving His people, she is showing love to Him.

The vines of the vineyard are coming alive unto the spring. The opening vines suggest that soon the grapes will form. Soon there will be a harvest of His suffering among these insignificant ones. The pomegranate again stands for righteousness. These, overlooked by the majority, will enter the fellowship of sharing in His suffering. His righteousness will be the result.

Insignificance Grows Big Hearts

An interesting point about those who huddle together in cities, in powerful positions, feeling important. Grapes and pomegranates are not grown in cities. Her fruit is grown in the villages among the insignificant ones. God is not looking for big names or big ministries. Rather, He is looking for big hearts. He wants hearts with a capacity to serve and love Him, forsaking all other gods and ideologies. People who feel wise and wonderful lack the capacity to love Him that way. If they let Him, He will break them, so they see their insignificance and thereby know Him in truth.

In this place among these hurting people, the bride gives Him her love. It is here that she fellowships with Him, and here that she loves Him by loving His people. The mature bride does not look for flashy ministry, and often is overlooked by those who are important, but the Lord does not overlook her. In our society, we think of the person with a small ministry or small church as having little success. This is not true. To die is to live in the Kingdom. So, failure in the eyes of men could be a success in God's eyes? For example, after tall, handsome Saul failed God as king, the Lord spoke these words to Samuel when he went to Jesse's house to anoint a new king in Saul's place.

I Samuel 16:7 'But the Lord said to Samuel, "Do not consider his appearance or his height, for I have rejected him. The Lord does not look at the things man looks at. Man, looks at the outward appearance, but the Lord looks at the heart."'

Those who love being important will never learn this lesson, but the unimportant are learning it. Popularity and power are not a blessing. This much sought-after prize keeps a believer in spiritual immaturity. The big-name believer may have the terminology right, so everyone thinks they are mature. They may even fool people for a long time, but God knows the truth. Someday soon, everyone else will know too.

Being Unimportant

It is better to be unimportant a long time before success comes to a person. Yes, we need people who minister from the Lord's heart. This person must guard their heart, for many a minister of the gospel has been seduced by success to build a kingdom to their own glory. That is not success. It is deception masquerading as success.

I Corinthians 1:27-29 shows the purpose of insignificant people. *"But God chose the foolish things of the world to shame the wise; God chose the weak things of the world to shame the strong. He chose the lowly things, and the despised things - and the things that are not - to nullify the things that are, so that no one may boast before Him."*

The strong man and the wise man boast before Him. So, He chose the foolish, the weak, the lowly, the despised, and the things that are not. The bride knows this because she is one of them. She knows His heart for the lowly and desires to be among them with Him. It is these insignificant lilies, (Song 2:2) which He spends His time with. It is there in that place she will give Him her love. Loving those who are His own is loving Him.

For Reflection:

1. In this passage, her ministry to others helps her connect intimately with the Lord. Will you give the Lord your love in this place of ministry to the insignificant?

2. Do you judge by appearances and end up hurt by those who appear to be mature?

3. What needs to change in your thinking patterns to stop this? Ask the Lord for insight.

Prayer

Lord, I so often have this backwards. Forgive me and show me the insignificant ones you are calling me to help. Remind me to meet you in the place of fellowship that only comes in the villages with those whom others overlook.

Help me remember though you live in heaven, you also live in me and are with me, closer than my own breath. I belong to you. Expand my understanding of these truths so I will desire you in the villages. Help me to fellowship with those you have called me to and, first, to fellowship with you.

Chapter 22

Persecution and Leaning

Tired of Jealousy and Envy

Song 8:1 "if only you were to me like a brother who was nursed at my mother's breasts! Then, if I found you outside and kissed you, no one would despise me."

The bride desires Him to be her actual brother, allowing her to show deep affection without facing persecution. If He were a brother by natural birth or a brother in the Lord, her life would be easier. If she displayed an intense love for her biological brother, others wouldn't become envious. They would not mind if she worshipped a brother in the church. Making others into celebrities who we sit on pedestals to receive our awe is acceptable. In culture, it is a plus to worship the personality ethic and cast aside living by the character ethic.

Many are offended, however, when His bride follows hard after Him. They are jealous of this deep love, but do nothing to nurture this in their own lives. When she finds Him and rejoices in His presence, they despise her. Jealous persecutors are not just a part of her past life. This kind of treatment will never be completely behind her. The difference lies in her response to them.

Song 8:2 "I would lead you and bring you to my mother's house – she who has taught me. I would give you spiced wine to drink, the nectar of my pomegranates."

This passage is most likely referring to her spiritual mother, the Church, although her natural mother could be included. The bride received instruction from both her natural and spiritual mother. The Church is the major arena in which the believer learns, though persecutors can be in our families. Often, this learning happens because trials come, and the bride must learn to respond properly to them.

The passage shows that jealous persecutors are constantly present. Though no longer their slave, it is easy to tire of their attitude.

The spiced wine and nectar of her pomegranates represent wine or a drink with His attributes. She has the fruitfulness of Calvary in her life she would like to give Him in her mother's house. This causes jealousy, so she keeps it for when they are alone. How sad the expression of a heart wholly devoted to the Lord causes such a reaction among some of His people and among our families. Nevertheless, persecutors are necessary for our personal growth. However, she longs to communicate openly with the Lord in the presence of His followers.

Leaning on His Right Arm

Song 8:3 "His left arm is under my head and his right arm embraces me."

The word arm or hand is often a symbol of power, (Psa. 60:5, Isa. 38:2). He is her protection because he is all-powerful. Many take offense at the bride's devotion, but the Lord is her covering and protection. He holds her head; her renewed mind, and that keeps her free of the fear that used to attack during her slave days. He responds to her desire to tell the world of her love by protecting her through His strong right hand. It is with His hand of power that He embraces her.

He also responds with power. The right hand is the stronger. *Isaiah 41:10 "I will uphold you with my right hand."* He protects her by covering her and He upholds her by His strength. At one time the persecution caused her to fold, but now she has allowed Him to be her help.

Song 8:4 "Daughters of Jerusalem, I charge you: Do not arouse or awaken love until it so desires."

Though this verse in NIV is attributed to the bride, the context suggests that the Bridegroom is speaking. It is love within the bride that must be awakened.

The bride experienced persecution, and during that, found His protection and strength. Yet, her desire for an end to the persecution keeps her from being awakened to more love. Her focus is on "if only". "If only" is one of the major snares for believers. It is fairy tale talk. This internal dialogue gets our focus off the Lord and onto a yearning that is impossible to realize. We want Prince Charming to make our problems go away and we will live "happily ever after". But, happiness is temporary and dependent on circumstances. Joy is found in Him and is not dependent on anything but His steadfastness and our trust.

He is not her brother in the sense she desires. He is God. The devotion she feels for Him and that makes others jealous, He deserves. Her love for Him knew no bounds. When we get our eyes on "if only", our eyes are off Him and we stop our progress in God until we let Him fill our vision. Then we must learn the lesson of the next verse:

The Choice

Song 8:5 "Who is this coming up from the desert leaning on her lover?"

The desert is a dry, solitary place. Her experience with those who despise her because of her love puts her back in the desert. Believers know the desert is not where you want to be. Or is it? When Jesus was here ministering among us, He spent much time in the wilderness communing with the Father and out of that ministering to the people, *Luke 4:42, Mark 1:45.*

The most important part of this passage is the word Lover, in KJV, Beloved. The center piece of understanding is that He is our Lover, our Beloved. We meet Him in the desert. He showed His passion for us by dying to set us free and make us His own. He serves us with red-hot love, and He calls us to love Him with red-hot passion rather than lukewarm "love". This calls for a reality check. Is our passion for our own way, for an answer, to leave the desert? If the emphasis is on our need, He is not our Lover. Our passion is directed to wanting our own way. This keeps us in the desert.

The word desert comes from the Hebrew word "midbar" meaning to drive. [xi] Often, we feel we were driven to the desert. We did not choose it. This same word means desert or pasture. In fact, unbelief makes it a desert, dry with no water. Trust makes it a pasture with food, water, and the glorious presence of the Bridegroom. If we focus on our need, or what we want, it will stay a desert. Focus on the Lover will turn it into a pasture. The choice is ours.

Psalm 84:6 "Passing through the Valley of Baca, they make it a spring." Baca means weeping. The mature bride passes through the valley of weeping and turns it into a spring, into a place of plenty. She is the enclosed spring, and the water of her life is for Him.

Isaiah 41:18 "I will turn the desert into pools of water and the parched ground into springs." Isaiah 35:6" Water will gush forth in the wilderness, and streams in the desert." The water of God is often found in the desert, and the barren place becomes a pasture.

Isaiah 43:18 "Forget the former things; do not dwell on the past. See, I am doing a new thing! Now it springs up; do you not perceive it?"

It is a matter of perception. We see desert. Since He is doing a new thing, we are in pasture. The past keeps us in the desert. We stay in a dry place with no food or water until we trust. To see the pasture, we must change our focus. If we focus on Him the desert, the Valley of Weeping will become a pasture with water where we feed. Disaster turns into blessing.

In the pasture, we fill up with what He provides, and the answer we seek becomes unimportant because of Him. Our need exists to lead us to Him. When we trust, we come up out of the desert leaning on Him. This speaks of a new maturity and new intimacy with her Lover.

The last time we were asked "who is this coming up from the desert?" it referred to the Lord when He went to Calvary. He came up as a column of smoke on His wedding day, *(Song of Songs 3:6)*. However, if He came from the desert to bring life to the world, our perception of the desert experience must change. The desert is as necessary to the growth of the believer as water is to sustain our body. The desert is the place where we learn to lie down our lives for His will.

Learning to rely on the Lord in the desert is a hard lesson. *Proverbs 3:5* illustrates this point. *"Trust in the Lord with all your heart and lean not on your own understanding: in all your ways acknowledge him and he will make your paths straight."*

The word trust means to run to for refuge or to hope. [xli] We are to run to Him for refuge with all our hearts. This is difficult if the heart is still crushed or broken. We must decide to trust with our whole heart. The rest of the verse shows us how.

The word acknowledge means to ascertain by seeing. We are to see Him in all our ways. We must turn our attention from our own ability fix things and focus on seeing Him amid our lives, amid our circumstances. Knowledge of what He is doing could be scarce. He is with us in ALL our ways.

Then, when our eyes are on Him, He will direct our paths. The word direct means, "to make straight the way, to make right, pleasant or prosperous". If we keep our eyes on Him, He will keep us on a straight path, and we will come into a pleasant and prosperous place. So, trust in Him, learning to lean on Him will bring us into a pleasant place. The trusting bride comes from this pasture.

The bride has been learning much. In this passage, she learned to come up from the desert leaning on her lover. She is not leaning on her own understanding. She is not trusting in herself. There is only one who covers her or uphold her. Leaning on Him in any circumstance is becoming a way of life. Even the persecutors have little power to draw her attention. It is persecution and trouble that have driven her to Him, so she will lean. Thank God for persecution and trouble.

Leaning

Familiar pain
you sweep across my soul
not a friend
not an enemy
a necessity.

No escape
from that which I need
though escape
I wish for
I yearn for.

But wait
in the distance I see
a desert cross
and one who died for me.

He has the strength
that I lack
the love

I need

I will lean on Him.

For Reflection:

1.Do you still have persecutors? What scriptures can you memorize to prepare for future trouble?

2.How can you experience the pasture rather than the desert? What is the next step?

3. What spiritual disciplines can you put in place to help you draw close to the Lord?

Prayer

Lord, help me draw close to you every day. Make your presence my continual place of rest. Help me trust in you. Lord, speak to my heart. Reveal Emanuel, as the One who is within me, who is with me. Open my capacity to know you this way, to dwell in your presence. Help me know you beyond knowing and to trust you beyond my ability to trust. Lord be my "everything".

Chapter 23

The Bridegroom's Love

The Church Birthed

You have probably noticed by now that we can attribute the different speeches in Song of Songs to different people depending on the version of the bible. The original manuscripts do not tell us this information. It is up to translators and readers to decide. Some expositors attributed this next passage to the bride and others have attributed it to no one. Yet other expositors believe the Bridegroom is speaking. That is my opinion as well for reasons that will become obvious below.

Song 8:5 "Under the apple tree I roused you; there your mother conceived you, there she who was in labor gave you birth."

In this verse, the bridegroom speaks of rousing her. He roused her under the apple tree. In Song 2:3 He is the one apple tree. The bride was birthed from His side at His death. There, her mother gave birth to her. The spirit of disobedience thought He was dead and without progeny. In reality, a multitude was born that day. When the bride needs to be roused to love, that is where He directs her. As she beholds the one fruit tree, her response is to awaken to love Him more. When she went through this latest contact with persecutors, she saw again the one fruit tree. Struggle is often the vehicle for seeing His sacrifice.

Notice she was conceived and born under that tree. In a few moments of time, the church was conceived and birthed. During the hours it took Him to die, all of this happened. Seeing this anew and afresh the bride cannot help responding with love.

Song 8:6 "Place me like a seal over your heart, like a seal on your arm; for love is as strong as death, its jealousy as unyielding as the grave. It burns like a blazing fire, like a mighty flame."

God sealed the love of the Bridegroom for the bride on His heart and His arm on Calvary. As the nails went into His wrist, the seal of His love was imprinted upon His holy arm. When the spear when in His side the seal of His love was inscribed, and the Church was birthed. This then must be the Bridegroom requesting of the Bride that she place Him as a seal on her heart and arm since He already sealed us on His. The heart stands for her love, and the arm, her strength, and works. She places Him as a seal on her love. This again is the garden locked up, the sealed fountain. Her strength and works or her ministry is to be sealed as well. Both her love and ministry are to be sealed, even when His presence is missing from her. Her ministry is to remain sealed until His second coming, as we will see in the last verse.

The seal is legal and binding like a signature. Only with a seal was an eastern document considered authentic. Further, the Lord sealed our covenant in His blood. He wants His bride to place Him as a seal upon her life, showing her authentic love for Him. Authentic love for Him can make her a target of persecution, but she must commit to this again and again.

There is an important reason for this, "for love is as strong as death, its jealousy as unyielding as the grave." Death is permanent concerning our sojourn in this earthly sphere. The strength of death is, therefore, immense. God's love is like that.

His love is a jealous love as unyielding as the grave. He requires we love only Him.

Exodus 34:14 "Do not worship any other God, for the Lord, whose name is Jealous, is a jealous God." He is jealous of our worship of other gods.

Deuteronomy 34:14 "For the Lord your God is a consuming fire, a jealous God." The consuming fire comes upon the life of those not faithful to Him and burns the dross, leaving only what is true to Him. His jealousy includes discipline for sin.

Ezekiel 8:3 "The Spirit lifted me up between earth and heaven and in visions of God he took me to Jerusalem, to the entrance of the north gate of the inner court, where the idol that provokes to jealousy stood." Verse six shows that the Lord was far from His sanctuary because of this idol that the Israelites had set up in His temple. In fact, God left the temple in Ezekiel chapters 8-10. The Babylonians destroyed the temple shortly thereafter.

His jealous love carries consequences when His people violate it. Consuming fire comes burning up everything not of Him. This happened when the Bride found herself in the tomb having lost everything. The consuming fire destroyed her ideals and expectations, so she will come alive unto the Lord and His truth.

In this verse, the Bridegroom is asking His bride to remain faithful as she was taught. In fact, if her heart is sealed only to Him, then her ministry will be pure. He is asking her to receive daily the reality of His sacrifice and the seal of His love for her represented by the cross. He is calling her daily to take up her cross and die to her own agenda, so He will live through her.

Song 8:7 "Many waters cannot quench love, rivers cannot wash it away. If one were to give all the wealth of his house for love, it would be utterly scorned."

Many waters cannot put out the fire of God's love. Even the wrath of God against Christ for our sin on Calvary could not stop His love for us. In fact, it was God's wrath against sin that proves

His love. The more men have tried to put it out, the hotter it has burned as He beholds the bride of His heart.

In *Song 6:9* the words *"perfect one, is unique"* mean, my "complete one is one". First, she is His "complete one"[xlii] She is also the only one. As the only bride, she is one. There is no longer double mindedness in her. Her heart and mind are one in Him. The bride company is of one mind. This is because the true bride keeps her eyes on Him and allows the Christ life to live through her.

Psa. 22:20 "Deliver my soul from the sword, my only life from the power of the dog." The words "only life" mean, "my only one". [xliii] This is a Messianic Psalm. The Lord speaks this same expression about the bride in *Song 6:9*. That suggests that the phrase "my only one" is speaking of His people.

When Christ made intercession for us on Calvary, He prayed to be delivered from death, "the power of the sword", and He prayed for us, His "only one", to be delivered from the power of the dogs. They considered a dog a fierce, cruel enemy because they often wandered about in packs and were known to attack. The Pharisees attacked the Lord like this. Because of His intercession for us, the wrath of God against our sin, the wrath that took His life, could not quench His love. In fact, amid wrath, He interceded for us not only through His death, but also through this messianic prayer as the Word of God became the sacrifice.

Such is the love of God that its fire cannot be quenched. Rivers cannot wash it away as they would wash away the things of this life. The love of God will remain when all else is gone.

God's love cannot be bought even though we were to give everything we own for it. To experience the fullness of His love, we say yes to the Lord. His salvation is by grace alone. The price of love was paid, the price of a perfect, spotless lamb.

> O Love that wilt not let me go,
> I rest my weary soul in thee;

I give thee back the life I owe,
That in thine ocean depths its flow
May richer, fuller be.

O light that followest all my way,
I yield my flickering torch to thee;
My heart restores its borrowed ray,
That in thy sunshine's blaze its day
May brighter, fairer be.

O Joy that seekest me through pain,
I cannot close my heart to thee;
I trace the rainbow through the rain,
And feel the promise is not vain,
That morn shall tearless be.

O Cross that liftest up my head,
I dare not ask to fly from thee;
I lay in dust, life's glory dead.
And from the ground there blossoms red
Life that shall endless be.
(George Matheson 1882, Public Domain)

His Seal

Sealed and set apart,
wholly and completely yours.
From the east to the west
you have separated my sins
from me.

Let me stand with unveiled face
beholding Your great love
overwhelmed by Your Glory.

Transform me
into Your image
with increasing glory
as I behold the Indescribable
the Wholly Other
who loves me!!

How could Glory die for this one?
How could The Transcendent live in me?
How could The Ineffable choose
the common
then transform
the common into the likeness of Glory?

Live through me, even me.
Shine through me your brightness
and transform the world around me
by Your Majesty.

Call me, seal me, overwhelm me.
Unite my heart
that I would be One with You
every moment of every day.

Search every dark corner and
fill them with your Brightness
and glorify your Great Name
in this bride.

Seal me.
Seal my heart to be only and always yours.
Seal my arm that no work of the flesh
would express itself through me.
Let all be you,

only you.

My life exchanged for yours.

Two lives expressed as One Glory.

© Debra Webster

For Reflection:

1. Have you placed Him as a seal on your heart? Talk to Him about this and listen for His voice to you about this. What stands in the way?

2. Have you placed Him as a seal on your arm? Are your works His works? Ask Him how your works can become His works.

3. What idols are you still serving? Ask the Lord to show you how to get free of their influence.

4. Are you willing to commit to receiving His jealous love?

Prayer

Lord, you alone know the extent of my idolatry. The picture of Ezekiel's temple is awful. That my internal life still has some idols is worse than awful. I am amazed that you died for me. I am amazed that you paid the price of your own precious life for me. And Lord, I am grateful. How wonderful that you should choose me. I am accepted and loved because of you.

Show me oh, Lord, the idols that provoke you that I might become free. Help me place you as a seal on my life. Let everything I do speak forth your glory. Purify the hidden corners of my temple. Purge the places with the idols that provoke you to jealousy. In your love, bring death to those things that keep me from you. Show the hindrances for what they are and transform me into a mirror image of you.

Chapter 24

Calvary's Finished Work

The Immature Sister

Song 8:8 "We have a young sister and her breasts are not yet grown. What shall we do for our sister on the day she is spoken for? "

This believer is not mature or ready for marriage to the Bridegroom, since the breasts of ministry are not grown. Will she work to win the approval with her charms, or will she be faithful to the Lord. Because of this, the friends wonder what to do on her betrothal day.

Purpose of the Wall

Song 8:9 "If she is a wall, we will build towers of silver on her. If she is a door, we will enclose her with panels of cedar."

The wall mentioned is a wall of protection, such as a fortress. So, she will become a garden that is locked up, a fountain that is sealed. The door is a swinging door. There is a question implied. Will this sister be flirtatious rather than a garden locked up unto the Lord?

If she is a wall, towers of silver will be built on her. Towers are again watchtowers from which to view the enemy. These towers are silver, which speak of redemption.

If she is a door, the friends will enclose her with panels of cedar. Cedar is His sinless humanity. An enclosed door cannot swing. In that case, He will surround her with His sinless sacrifice to keep her from being a swinging door.

Then there are two types of believers. Some heed the call to intercession, fidelity, and intimacy. The others are flirtatious. They flirt with the world. These will be surrounded with His sinless sacrifice until they learn to lead a more circumspect life, until they become walls. The flirtatious are the slaves of the first chapter. This mature bride is called to help these flirtatious believers see the other way.

The bride we have followed through this book was once flirtatious. She used methods of behavior to gain approval. Those methods made her a slave. Because of this, she was enclosed with His sinless humanity as she beheld His table, and as she wore the myrrh between her breasts. He showed her that His sacrifice was her wedding price many times throughout this song. Her response was to become a garden locked up, a wall. The lessons she has learned are now to be shared with those who struggle with fidelity, so they will become as she is, totally focused on her beloved.

The Bride's Wall

Song 8:10 "I am a wall, and my breasts are like towers. Thus, I have become in his eyes like one bringing contentment." The bride is a wall with silver towers. She is faithful to the Lord alone. Peace is one way to understand the word contentment. She is a peacemaker among the Lord's people. She is content in His presence.

The Lord is the source of hope for the flirtatious, the religious addict, and those who appear irreparably broken. The broken will transform into a locked garden at a quicker pace if our ministry remains centered on Him.

He is the one who died. History revolves around his cross. He was sinless and loved us. He calls us to daily crucifixion, to die to our will and become alive to His. Everything else we do must be considering these truths. If we will lift Him up among us, if we emphasize His finished work on behalf of our fidelity, a mighty restoration will come to the bride.

His Vineyard

Song *8:11 "Solomon had a vineyard in Baal Hamon; he let out his vineyard to tenants. Each was to bring for its fruit a thousand shekels of silver."*

Baal Hamon means, lord of a multitude. That is the Church. The Lord asks believers to tend various vineyards. Each is to bring the profit to Him. When we minister, we are to give to the Lord the praise and adulation of the people. It's fine to acknowledge that the ministry was helpful to them, but it's not beneficial to seek praise and adulation for us.

Matthew 22:33 tells us a story of tenants who tended the Lord's vineyard. They kept the profit for themselves. The Lord sent messengers, prophets to them and they beat and killed them. In the end, He sent His beloved son, but they murdered Him, plotting to claim the inheritance. Their fate is in verse 41: *"He will bring those wretches to a wretched end,"* they replied, "and he will rent the vineyard to other tenants, who will give him his share of the crop at harvest time."

It is dangerous to keep what belongs to the Lord. Verse 43, *"Therefore I tell you that the Kingdom of God will be taken away from you and given to a people who will produce its fruit."*

The Jewish people forfeited the Kingdom, and it was given to the gentiles and any person who believed in the Messiah. No longer were they the only covenant people. Both Jews and non-Jews must now have faith in Jesus.

So, the praise and glory belong to Him. Indeed, those who take care of the vineyard and harvest its fruits will give Him the praise and glory that He deserves. They do not keep this precious fruit for themselves. They are humble and obedient keepers and tend the fruit with great care.

Song 8:12 "But my own vineyard is mine to give; the thousand shekels are for you, O Solomon, and two hundred are for those who tend its fruit."

Because of growth, the bride is now tending her own vineyard. No longer in slavery under her brothers, she has abundant fruitfulness. She gives to the Lord His due, not because she owes Him, but because He deserves it. Then she pays the workers. These labor with her in ministry. They are not slaves.

Song 8:13 "You who dwell in the gardens with friends in attendance, let me hear your voice!

King James version renders this passage: *"Thou that dwellest in the gardens, the companions hearken to thy voice: cause me to hear it."*

A study in the original Hebrew confirms the friends are hearing the voice of the bride. So, the bride company talks to one another and encourages one another. This is a picture of fellowship among His Bride. When His people come together, He wants to hear their voices rise as one voice before Him. Such is the unity they enjoy because they have submitted to the process of His song. He desires to hear not only the corporate bride. He desires to hear you.

Song 8:14 "Come away my lover, and be like a gazelle or a young stag on the spice-laden mountains.

When the bride causes Him to hear her voice, there is not only praise and adoration but also the desire for His return. The spice-laden mountains signify the finished work of Calvary. His bride longs for the day when she will know the fullness of life with Him. The united company of His people minister here in the earth with an eye toward heaven.

Revelation 22:17, 20 'The Spirit and the bride say, "Come!" He who testifies to these things says, "Yes, I am coming soon." Amen come Lord Jesus.'

For Reflection:

1.Will you accept the challenge to help enclose those who are not yet mature?

2. Will you help others understand we are called to the fidelity of the locked garden?

3. Do you commit yourself to the Lord and to His people in such a way that you will determine to follow Him and love His people, no matter the cost?

4. How can you live so others will long for Him too? Let Him speak this to your heart.

Prayer

Precious Bridegroom Lamb. There is only one reason to say yes to these questions. That reason is love of you. Help me remember the many lessons your song teaches. Help me grow in a way that glorifies you. Let me be a wall, a garden locked unto you. Work in me the lessons needed to bring me to the singleness of heart I need. Show me how to give you the glory. Teach me what true obedience is. Draw me, Lord, and continue to draw me until I am completely yours.

.

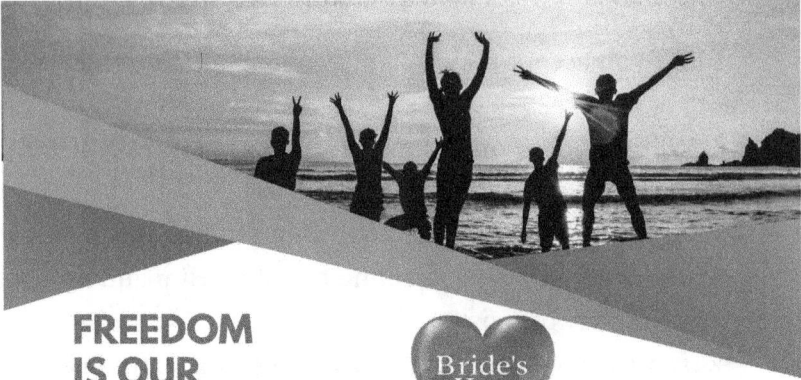

FREEDOM
IS OUR
BIRTHRIGHT

Bride's Heart
Becoming The Bride Of Christ

5 STEPS TO A TRANSFORMED MIND

GAL. 5:1 FOR FREEDOM CHRIST HAS SET US FREE

Get a free book, read blogs and other goodies.

https://www.bridesheart.com/

About the Author

Debra Webster has served the Lord in ministry since 1972. She and her husband attended Melodyland School of Theology in Anaheim, California and Elim Bible Institute in upper New York State. She has been a speaker, bible teacher and mentor for the last 40+ years.

Debra has written:

- *Bridegroom's Song* is an exposition of Song of Songs illustrating the Bridegroom's love and the bride's response.

- *For the Bride* is a devotional to help the bride grow close to the Lord.
- *His Bride has Made Herself Ready* helps the bride know how to get ready for her Bridegroom.
- *Mystery Bride and Mystery Babylon* illustrates the difference between the Bride and the harlot and principles of getting ready for the Bridegroom. It is an expansion on *His Bride has* Made Herself Ready.
- *From Shame's Prison to Joy* book and workbook take the Lord's Bride from shame and fear to a life of joy in Christ so she can serve him with her whole heart.
- Cracking the Bridal Code to Transformation-From Genesis to Exodus God's Heart is Set on a Bride. This is Her Story.

Debra coaches those who need freedom. Contact her through her website or e-mail. Visit her author page to read about her books.

e-mail: **dg_webster@att.net**

Website: **https://bridesheart.com**

http://www.amazon.com/author/debrawebster

End Notes

Chapter 2
[i] Strong's Hebrew Chaldee Dictionary of Old Testament Words, Public Domain
[ii] Ibid.
[iii]*Ibid*, 590

Chapter 8
[iv]Strong's Greek Dictionary of the New Testament, Public Domain
[v] Ibid.
[vi] Ibid.

vii Ibid.
viii Ibid
ix Ibid.

Chapter 10

xi Strong's Greek Dictionary of the New Testament, Public
Domain
xii Webster's New Collegiate Dictionary, Public Domain
xiiiStrong's Dictionary of New Testament Words, Public Domain

Chapter 11
xivStrong's Hebrew Chaldee Dictionary of Old Testament
Words, Public Domain.

Chapter 13
xv The New Unger's Bible Dictionary by Merrill F. Unger. R. K.
Harrison, editor. Used by permission of Moody Bible Institute
of Chicago. All rights reserved.

Chapter 15
xviThe New Unger's Bible Dictionary by Merrill F. Unger. R. K.
Harrison, editor. Used by permission of Moody Bible Institute
of Chicago. All rights reserved.
xvii Ibid.
xvii Ibid.
xix

xx NIV Dictionary New American Standard Bible
Update,Copyright ©1960, 1962, 1963,1968, 1971, 1972, 1973,
1975, 1977, 1995 by The LockmanFoundation,All rights
reserved, New American Standard Bible, 1995 edition, with
Strong's numbers.Version 3.7
xxi Ibid.
xxii Ibid.
xxiiiThe New Unger's Bible Dictionary by Merrill F. Unger.R. K.
Harrison, editor. Used by permission of Moody Bible Institute
of Chicago. All rights reserved.
xxiv Ibid.

Chapter 16
xxv The New Unger's Bible Dictionary by Merrill F. Unger.R. K.
Harrison, editor. Used by permission of Moody Bible Institute
of Chicago. All rights reserved.

[xxvi] Strong's Hebrew Chaldee Dictionary of the Old Testament, Public Domain

Chapter 17
[xxvii] Wigram's Hebrew Word Parsings, Public Domain,
[xxviii] Strong's Hebrew Chaldee Dictionary of Old Testament Words, Public Domain
[xxix] Ibid,
[xxx] Ibid.

Chapter 18
[xxxi] New American Standard Bible Update, Copyright ©1960, 1962, 1963, 1968, 1971, 1972, 1973, 1975, 1977, 1995 by the Lockman Foundation, All right reserved, New American Standard Bible, 1995 edition, with Strong's numbers
[xxxii] Strong's Hebrew Chaldee Dictionary of Old Testament Words, Public Domain
[xxxiii] Ibid.
[xxxiv] Ibid.

Chapter 19
[xxxv] Strong's Hebrew Chaldee Dictionary of Old Testament Words, Public Domain
[xxxvi] Ibid.
[xxxvii] Ibid.

Chapter 20
[xxxviii] Strong's Hebrew Chaldee Dictionary of Old Testament Words, Public Domain
[xxxix] Ibid.

Chapter 22
[xxxix] Strong's Hebrew Chaldee Dictionary of Old Testament Words, Public Domain
[xxxix] Ibid.
[xli] Ibid

Chapter 23
[xlii] Strong's Hebrew Chaldee Dictionary of Old Testament Words, Public Domain
[xliii] Ibid.

www.ingramcontent.com/pod-product-compliance
Lightning Source LLC
LaVergne TN
LVHW051226080426
835513LV00016B/1429